Richard Dembo, PhD
Nathaniel J. Pallone, PhD
Editors

FAMILY EMPOWERMENT AS AN INTERVENTION STRATEGY IN JUVENILE DELINQUENCY

Family Empowerment as an Intervention Strategy in Juvenile Delinquency has been co-published simultaneously as *Journal of Offender Rehabilitation*, Volume 33, Number 1 2001.

Pre-publication
REVIEWS,
COMMENTARIES,
EVALUATIONS . . .

" A hands-on book. . . . Provides detailed guidelines for counselors regarding implementation of the FEI curriculum . . . accurately describes the scope of counselor responsibilities and the nature of treatment interventions. Unique in its coverage of counselor competencies and training/supervision needs. Innovative and based on solid empirical evidence."

Roger H. Peters, PhD
Professor, Department of Mental Health Law and Policy, Louis de la Parte Florida Mental Health Institute University of South Florida, Tampa

FAMILY EMPOWERMENT
AS AN INTERVENTION
STRATEGY
IN JUVENILE DELINQUENCY

Family Empowerment as an Intervention Strategy in Juvenile Delinquency has been co-published simultaneously as *Journal of Offender Rehabilitation*, Volume 33, Number 1 2001.

The *Journal of Offender Rehabilitation* Monographic "Separates"

Below is a list of "separates," which in serials librarianship means a special issue simultaneously published as a special journal issue or double-issue *and* as a "separate" hardbound monograph. (This is a format which we also call a "DocuSerial.")

"Separates" are published because specialized libraries or professionals may wish to purchase a specific thematic issue by itself in a format which can be separately cataloged and shelved, as opposed to purchasing the journal on an on-going basis. Faculty members may also more easily consider a "separate" for classroom adoption.

"Separates" are carefully classified separately with the major book jobbers so that the journal tie-in can be noted on new book order slips to avoid duplicate purchasing.

You may wish to visit Haworth's website at . . .

http://www.HaworthPress.com

. . . to search our online catalog for complete tables of contents of these separates and related publications.

You may also call 1-800-HAWORTH (outside US/Canada: 607-722-5857), or Fax 1-800-895-0582 (outside US/Canada: 607-771-0012), or e-mail at:

getinfo@haworthpressinc.com

Family Empowerment as an Intervention Strategy in Juvenile Delinquency, edited by Richard Dembo, PhD, and Nathaniel J. Pallone, PhD (Vol. 33, No. 1, 2001). *"A hands-on book. . . . Provides detailed guidelines for counselors regarding implementation of the FEI curriculum . . . accurately describes the scope of counselor responsibilities and the nature of treatment interventions. Unique in its coverage of counselor competencies and training/supervision needs. Innovative and based on solid empirical evidence." (Roger H. Peters, PhD, Professor, University of South Florida, Tampa)*

Race, Ethnicity, Sexual Orientation, Violent Crime: The Realities and the Myths, edited by Nathaniel J. Pallone, PhD (Vol. 30, No. 1/2, 1999). *"A fascinating book which illuminates the complexity of race as it applies to the criminal justice system and the myths and political correctness that have shrouded the real truth. . . . I highly recommend this book for those who study causes of crime in minority populations." (Joseph R. Carlson, PhD, Associate Professor, University of Nebraska at Kearney)*

Sex Offender Treatment: Biological Dysfunction, Intrapsychic Conflict, Interpersonal Violence, edited by Eli Coleman, PhD, S. Margretta Dwyer, MA, and Nathaniel J. Pallone, PhD (Vol. 23, No. 3/4, 1996). *"Offers a review of current assessment and treatment theory while addressing critical issues such as standards of care, use of phallometry, and working with specialized populations such as exhibitionists and developmentally disabled clients. . . . A valuable addition to the reader's professional library." (Robert E. Freeman-Longo, MRC, LPC, Director, The Safer Society Press)*

The Psychobiology of Aggression: Engines, Measurement, Control, edited by Marc Hillbrand, PhD, and Nathaniel J. Pallone, PhD (Vol. 21, No. 3/4, 1994). *"A comprehensive sourcebook for the increasing dialogue between psychobiologists, neuropsychiatrists, and those interested in a full understanding of the dynamics and control of criminal aggression." (Criminal Justice Review)*

Young Victims, Young Offenders: Current Issues in Policy and Treatment, edited by Nathaniel J. Pallone, PhD (Vol. 21, No. 1/2, 1994). *"Extremely practical. . . . Aims to increase knowledge about the patterns of youthful offenders and give help in designing programs of prevention and rehabilitation." (S. Margretta Dwyer, Director of Sex Offender Treatment Program, Department of Family Practice, University of Minnesota)*

Sex Offender Treatment: Psychological and Medical Approaches, edited by Eli Coleman, PhD, S. Margretta Dwyer, and Nathaniel J. Pallone, PhD (Vol. 18, No. 3/4, 1992). *"Summarizes research worldwide on the various approaches to treating sex offenders for both researchers and clinicians." (SciTech Book News)*

The Clinical Treatment of the Criminal Offender in Outpatient Mental Health Settings: New and Emerging Perspectives, edited by Sol Chaneles, PhD, and Nathaniel J. Pallone, PhD (Vol. 15, No. 1, 1990). *"The clinical professional concerned with the outpatient treatment of the criminal offender will find this book informative and useful." (Criminal Justice Review)*

Older Offenders: Current Trends, edited by Sol Chaneles, PhD, and Cathleen Burnett, PhD (Vol. 13, No. 2, 1985). *"Broad in scope and should provide a fruitful beginning for future discussion and exploration." (Criminal Justice Review)*

Prisons and Prisoners: Historical Documents, edited by Sol Chaneles, PhD (Vol. 10, No. 1/2, 1985). *"May help all of us . . . to gain some understanding as to why prisons have resisted change for over 300 years. . . . Very challenging and very disturbing." (Public Offender Counseling Association)*

Gender Issues, Sex Offenses, and Criminal Justice: Current Trends, edited by Sol Chaneles, PhD (Vol. 9, No. 1/2, 1984). *"The contributions of the work will be readily apparent to any reader interested in an interdisciplinary approach to criminology and women's studies." (Criminal Justice Review)*

Current Trends in Correctional Education: Theory and Practice, edited by Sol Chaneles, PhD (Vol. 7, No. 3/4, 1983). *"A laudable presentation of educational issues in relation to corrections." (International Journal of Offender Therapy and Comparative Criminology)*

Counseling Juvenile Offenders in Institutional Settings, edited by Sol Chaneles, PhD (Vol. 6, No. 3, 1983). *"Covers a variety of settings and approaches, from juvenile awareness programs, day care, and vocational rehabilitation to actual incarceration in juvenile and adult institutions. . . . Good coverage of the subject." (Canada's Mental Health)*

Strategies of Intervention with Public Offenders, edited by Sol Chaneles, PhD (Vol. 6, No. 1/2, 1982). *"The information presented is well-organized and should prove useful to the practitioner, the student, or for use in in-service training." (The Police Chief)*

FAMILY EMPOWERMENT AS AN INTERVENTION STRATEGY IN JUVENILE DELINQUENCY

Richard Dembo, PhD
Nathaniel J. Pallone, PhD
Editors

Family Empowerment as an Intervention Strategy in Juvenile Delinquency has been co-published simultaneously as *Journal of Offender Rehabilitation*, Volume 33, Number 1 2001.

The Haworth Press, Inc.
New York • London • Oxford

Family Empowerment as an Intervention Strategy in Juvenile Delinquency has been co-published simultaneously as *Journal of Offender Rehabilitation*, Volume 33, Number 1 2001.

Cover design by Thomas J. Mayshock Jr.

Library of Congress Cataloging-in-Publication Data

Family empowerment as an intervention strategy in juvenile delinquency / Richard Dembo, Nathaniel J. Pallone, editors.
    p. cm.
    Co-published simultaneously as Journal of offender rehabilitation, volume 33, numbers 1 2001."
    Includes bibliographical references and index.
    ISBN 0-7890-1390-8 (alk. paper) -- ISBN 0-7890-1391-6 (alk. paper)
    1. Juvenile delinquents-Family relationships. 2. Juvenile delinquency-Prevention. 3. Juvenile delinquents-Rehabilitation. 4. Social control. I. Dembo, Richard. II. Pallone, Nathaniel J. III. Journal of offender rehabilitation.

HV9085 .F36 2001
364.36´-dc21
    2001039429

Indexing, Abstracting & Website/Internet Coverage

This section provides you with a list of major indexing & abstracting services. That is to say, each service began covering this periodical during the year noted in the right column. Most Websites which are listed below have indicated that they will either post, disseminate, compile, archive, cite or alert their own Website users with research-based content from this work. (This list is as current as the copyright date of this publication.)

(continued)

Special Bibliographic Notes related to special journal issues (separates) and indexing/abstracting:

- indexing/abstracting services in this list will also cover material in any "separate" that is co-published simultaneously with Haworth's special thematic journal issue or DocuSerial. Indexing/abstracting usually covers material at the article/chapter level.
- monographic co-editions are intended for either non-subscribers or libraries which intend to purchase a second copy for their circulating collections.
- monographic co-editions are reported to all jobbers/wholesalers/approval plans. The source journal is listed as the "series" to assist the prevention of duplicate purchasing in the same manner utilized for books-in-series.
- to facilitate user/access services all indexing/abstracting services are encouraged to utilize the co-indexing entry note indicated at the bottom of the first page of each article/chapter/contribution.
- this is intended to assist a library user of any reference tool (whether print, electronic, online, or CD-ROM) to locate the monographic version if the library has purchased this version but not a subscription to the source journal.
- individual articles/chapters in any Haworth publication are also available through the Haworth Document Delivery Service (HDDS).

FAMILY EMPOWERMENT AS AN INTERVENTION STRATEGY IN JUVENILE DELINQUENCY

CONTENTS

RICHARD DEMBO

Department of Criminology, University of South Florida, Tampa

GARY DUDELL

*Department of Rehabilitation and Mental Health Counseling,
University of South Florida, Tampa*

STEPHEN LIVINGSTON

Department of Criminology, University of South Florida, Tampa

JAMES SCHMEIDLER

*Departments of Psychiatry and Biomathematical Sciences,
Mt. Sinai School of Medicine, New York*

RICHARD DEMBO

Department of Criminology, University of South Florida, Tampa

GABRIELA RAMIREZ-GARNICA

*Department of Epidemiology and Biostatistics, University of South Florida,
Tampa*

JAMES SCHMEIDLER

*Departments of Psychiatry and Biomathematical Sciences,
Mt. Sinai School of Medicine, New York*

MATTHEW ROLLIE

*Department of Environmental and Occupational Health,
University of South Florida, Tampa*

STEPHEN LIVINGSTON

Department of Criminology, University of South Florida, Tampa

AMY HARTSFIELD

Department of Criminology, University of South Florida, Tampa

RICHARD DEMBO

Department of Criminology, University of South Florida, Tampa

JAMES SCHMEIDLER

*Departments of Psychiatry and Biomathematical Sciences,
Mt. Sinai School of Medicine, New York*

WILLIAM SEEBERGER

Department of Criminology, University of South Florida, Tampa

MARINA SHEMWELL

Department of Criminology, University of South Florida, Tampa

MATTHEW ROLLIE

*Department of Environmental and Occupational Health,
University of South Florida, Tampa*

KIMBERLY PACHECO

Department of Criminology, University of South Florida, Tampa

STEPHEN LIVINGSTON

Department of Criminology, University of South Florida, Tampa

WERNER WOTHKE

Small Waters Corporation, Chicago

ABOUT THE EDITORS

Richard Dembo, PhD, is Professor of Criminology at the University of South Florida in Tampa. He received his PhD in sociology from New York University. He has conducted extensive research on the relationship between drug use and delinquency; has published a book and over 150 articles, book chapters, and reports in the fields of criminology, substance use, mental health, and program evaluation; and has guest edited five special issues of journals addressing the problem of drug misuse. He is a member of the editorial boards of *The International Journal of the Addictions* (recently renamed *Journal of Drug Issues*) and the *Journal of Child and Adolescent Substance Abuse*. He has served as a consultant to the National Institute of Justice, the Office of Juvenile Justice and Delinquency Prevention, the National Institute on Drug Abuse, the National Institute of Mental Health, the Center for Substance Abuse Treatment, the Office of Substance Abuse Prevention, and the National Science Foundation; and he is a reviewer of manuscripts for numerous professional journals. He is Past-Chair of the American Sociological Association Section on Alcohol and Drugs. He has extensive experience working with troubled youths in a variety of settings and in applying research technology to social problems. He is currently working on a NIDA funded experimental, longitudinal service delivery project designed to implement and test a Family Empowerment Intervention involving high risk youths and their families; and is Research director of the Miami-Dade Juvenile Assessment Center, National Demonstration Project. He helped develop the Hillsborough County Juvenile Assessment Center in Tampa and supports JAC operations by: (1) completing special research studies and (2) developing, implementing, and evaluating the impact of innovative service delivery projects for youths processed at the JAC and their families. He has been a major party in the flow of millions of dollars in federal, state, and local funds into the University of South Florida and the Tampa Bay area for various research and service delivery projects addressing the needs of high risk youths, their families, and their surrounding communities.

Nathaniel J. Pallone, PhD, Editor-in-Chief of the *Journal of Offender Rehabilitation*, is University Distinguished Professor (Psychology), Center of Alcohol Studies, at Rutgers–The State University of New Jersey, where he previously served as Dean and as Academic Vice President.

Family Empowerment as an Intervention Strategy in Juvenile Delinquency. Pp. xiii-xv.

Preface

This volume is devoted to a Family Empowerment Intervention (FEI) for juvenile offenders and their families. Arrested youths processed at the Hillsborough County Juvenile Assessment Center and their families were enrolled in this voluntary project over a three-year period. The FEI was implemented as part of a National Institute on Drug Abuse funded, Youth Support Project (YSP). The YSP was an innovative, large-scale, experimental, prospective longitudinal study, involving baseline and up to three follow-up interview data collection waves and recidivism analyses. Families involved in the project were randomly assigned to one of two groups: (1) Extended Services Intervention (ESI) or the FEI group. ESI group families received monthly telephone contacts from project research staff and, if indicated, referral information. FEI families received personal, in-home services from project Field Consultants who worked with assigned families on nine project goals. These goals are described in the first article in this special issue, which reviews the conceptual foundations and clinical practices of the FEI. A distinctive feature of the FEI was that the FCs were not trained therapists-although they were trained by, and performed their work under the direction of, licensed clinicians. This feature reduced the cost of providing intervention services considerably. The major hypothesis of the YSP was that empowering parents would reduce target youth recidivism and increase target youth prosocial behavior and psychosocial functioning.

In addition to discussing the goals of the FEI, the conceptual foundations and clinical practices article presents: the structural intervention strategies used in working the FEI families; the phases of the intervention; engaging and moving families through the intervention to graduation; the role, and selection and training of the FCs delivering the intervention; efforts to ensure the integrity of intervention services; crisis intervention procedures; and staff and family safety issues. The article provides a fairly detailed overview of the nature, purposes, and activities involved in the FEI.

Previous reports of this study, focusing on 12-month outcomes, indicated the salutary effect of the FEI on youth recidivism (Dembo, Ramirez-Garnica et al., 2000) and their psychosocial functioning (Dembo, Seeberger et al., 2000). The two outcome papers included in this volume document the long-term impact of the FEI on target youth functioning in each of these two domains.

The first of the two long-term outcome papers focuses on the youths' new charges and new arrests. The data reported include all 303 youths entering the YSP during the period September 1, 1994 to December 31, 1997. Depending on the year in which youths entered the project, cumulative new charge and arrest information were collected from 12 to 48 months following random assignment to the 10-week FEI or the ESI group. The results presented in this paper indicate that youths who completed the FEI experienced marginally statistically significant, lower rates of new charges and very close to statistically significant, lower rates of new arrests than youths who did not complete the FEI. The results provide evidence for the sustained deterrent effects of the FEI on recidivism. Since the FEI was designed to be short-term, and no additional services were systematically applied following completion of the FEI, these long-term effects were gratifying.

The second outcome article in this special issue reports the results of analyses of the long-term impact of the FEI on the psychosocial functioning of youths entering the YSP between September 1, 1994 and January 31, 1998. Depending on the year in which youths entered the project, up to three annual follow-up interviews were completed. The results provide additional evidence in support of the sustained effects of FEI services. Analyses indicated that youths who completed the intervention had statistically significant, lower rates of getting very high or drunk on alcohol, and claimed less frequency of participation in crimes against persons, drug sales, and total delinquency at last observation, than youths not completing the FEI.

The Youth Support Project was a demanding, growth-filled experience for me and other project staff. Quality intervention services were needed. Over 850 in-depth interviews were completed with the youths involved in the various analyses. Tracking and completing follow-up interviews with them and their families often involved creativity and persistence. This project could not have been completed without the support of caring, dedicated staff.

Clinical, intervention and project research staff are to be deeply thanked for their contributions to the success of this project. Project Field Consultants are particularly deserving of appreciation. The Agency for Community Treatment Services, Inc. was a consistent supporter of our work, as was the Hillsborough County Sheriffs Office, the Hillsborough County School Board, the Florida

Department of Juvenile Justice, and the Florida Department of Corrections. The National Institute on Drug Abuse staff, particularly Dr. Peter Delany and Dr. Jerry Flanzer, deserve special thanks for their support. I wish also to thank the many youths and families we served for their trust and for the privilege of working with them.

Finally, I should like to publicly express my heartfelt appreciation to my wife, Enid. Her patience with the long hours and often weekends of work needed to complete this project, and the many evenings I returned home late after conducting interviews, was an essential factor in the project's success. I truly believe that this project could not have been completed without her wisdom, advice, and support.

Richard Dembo
5/19/2001

REFERENCES

Richard Dembo, Gabriela Ramirez-Garnica, Matthew Rollie, James Schmeidler, Stephen Livingston, & Amy Hartsfleld (2000). "Youth recidivism 12 months after a family empowerment intervention: Final Report." *Journal of Offender Rehabilitation,* 31, 29-65.

Richard Dembo, William Seeberger, Marina Shemwell, James Schmeidler, Matthew Rollie, Kimberly Pacheco, Amy Hartsfield, & Werner Wothke (2000). "Psychosocial functioning among juvenile offenders 12 months after Family Empowerment Intervention." *Journal of Offender Rehabilitation,* 32, 1-56.

Family Empowerment as an Intervention Strategy in Juvenile Delinquency. Pp. 1-31.
© *2001 by The Haworth Press, Inc. All rights reserved.*

Family Empowerment Intervention: Conceptual Foundations and Clinical Practices

RICHARD DEMBO

Department of Criminology, University of South Florida, Tampa

GARY DUDELL

Department of Rehabilitation and Mental Health Counseling, University of South Florida, Tampa

STEPHEN LIVINGSTON

Department of Criminology, University of South Florida, Tampa

JAMES SCHMEIDLER

Departments of Psychiatry and Biomathematical Sciences, Mt. Sinai School of Medicine, New York

ABSTRACT This article presents a detailed overview of the Family Empowerment Intervention (FEI), a systems-oriented intervention delivered in-home by well-trained nontherapists. A clinical trial of the FEI, funded by the National Institute on Drug Abuse, targeted arrested youths and their families. The following topics are covered: the theoretical foundations of the FEI; the goals of the FEI; structural intervention strategies; the phases of the intervention; engaging and moving families through the FEI to graduation; the role, selection, and training of Field Consultants who deliver the intervention; efforts to ensure the integrity of intervention services; crisis intervention; and staff and family safety issues. *[Article copies available for a fee from The Haworth Document Delivery Service: 1-800-342-9678. E-mail address: <getinfo@ haworthpressinc.com> Website: <http://www.HaworthPress.com> © 2001 by The Haworth Press, Inc. All rights reserved.]*

KEYWORDS Juvenile offender family intervention, family empowerment intervention for high-risk youths, family empowerment intervention conceptual foundations

INTRODUCTION

Treatment of adolescents for alcohol/other drug abuse and related problems in the juvenile justice system remains an issue of critical importance for several reasons. First, there has been an increase in youth crime and its effects, as well as a growing awareness of the magnitude of these and related problems among various high-risk groups (Butts & Harrell, 1998). This increase, together with a higher rate of law violation referrals to juvenile court (a 57% increase between 1980 and 1995), has resulted in an increasingly clogged and backlogged juvenile court system and less involvement in case deliberation (Snyder & Sickmund, 1995). Younger offenders are entering the juvenile system in increasing numbers and are bringing with them a number of serious, interrelated problems–including drug use, educational deficits and emotional/psychological issues (including abuse and neglect) (Dembo, Schmeidler, Nini-Gough et al., 1998). Further, demographic projections indicate a substantial increase in the U.S. youth population in the next 10 to 20 years, which threatens to create an increasingly overburdened juvenile justice system. Second, drug testing results from national studies (National Institute of Justice, 1999) of juvenile arrestees indicate continuing high levels of drug use. Third, evidence indicates an increased co-occurrence of mental health and drug abuse problems among juvenile offenders (Winters, 1998).

A knowledge base deriving from experience in treating youths has begun to be established. However, rigorous, comprehensive impact and cost studies of treatment interventions in the juvenile justice system remain relatively infrequent. Rates of failure of adolescents to enter and remain in treatment present continuing challenges to service delivery (Battjes, Onken, & Delany, 1999). Many drug-involved youths do not enter treatment or leave prematurely, with associated high rates of return to drug use, involvement in crime, increased risk of HIV/AIDS, and other health and social problems. Post-treatment relapse rates among adolescents with drug abuse problems (Catelano, Hawkins, Wells et al., 1990-1991), particularly those involved in the justice system, remain high (Armstrong & Altschuler, 1998), reflecting the often chronic nature of these problems.

Many youths entering the juvenile justice system have multiple personal, educational, and family problems. These problems include physical abuse, sexual victimization, emotional/psychological functioning difficulties, educational problems, and alcohol and other drug use (Dembo, Williams, & Schmeidler, 1998). These youths' difficulties can often be traced to family alcohol/other drug use, mental health, or crime problems which began at an early age (Dembo, Williams, Wothke et al., 1992). One in four U.S. children, or 19 million, is exposed to alcohol abuse or dependence at home before reaching the age of 18 (Grant, 2000).

Identifying and responding effectively to these youths' drug abuse and related problems as early as possible by involving them in effective intervention services (Klitzner, Fisher, Stewart et al., 1991) would reduce: (1) the risk of their types and patterns of drug use and related problems escalating (especially crime: Anglin & Speckart, 1988; Dembo, Ramirez-Garnica et al., in press a, b), (2) their moving into the adult criminal justice system, and (3) the enormous cost to our society of crime, drug abuse, and mental illness (Institute for Health Policy, 1993; Office of National Drug Control Policy, 1997). Innovative services are especially needed by minority and inner city youths and their families, who have historically been underserved (Arcia, Keyes, Gallagher et al., 1993; Dembo & Seeberger, 1999).

Family interventions, delivered to at-risk youths at the point of early contact with the justice system, are particularly well suited to address youths' needs in a holistic manner. In response to these needs, several community-based family interventions, informed by an ecological systems view, are being implemented in various parts of the U.S. (e.g., Rahdert & Czechowicz, 1995; Kumpfer & Alvarado, 1998). For example, multisystemic therapy (MST) has been found successful in addressing the needs of noninstitutionalized juvenile delinquent and drug-using offenders and their families (Henggeler, Schoenwald, Pickrel et al., 1994; Henggeler, Pickrel, Brondino et al., 1996; Henggeler, 1997). Trained therapists at community mental health centers provided services to four to six "at-risk youths" and their families for as long as four to five months. Based on a structural family therapy perspective, the first step is to develop parental competencies in order to restructure the family and establish parental control. A second goal is to teach the parents how to use agencies and services, including schools, more effectively (Henggeler, Schoenwald, Pickrel et al., 1994).

Functional family therapy (Alexander & Parsons, 1982) has also been found effective in treating youths 11 to 18 years of age who are involved in alcohol or other drug abuse or delinquent behavior, and in reducing justice and other service system costs in serving these youths. A wide range of trained interventionists work in one or two person teams. They provide from 8 to 26 hours of in-home services to referred youths and their families. This treatment has five phases: engagement, motivation, assessment, behavior change, and generalization.

The Youth Support Project (YSP), a National Institute on Drug Abuse (NIDA) funded family intervention project, implemented a systems-oriented, home-based Family Empowerment Intervention (FEI). The FEI ideally takes ten weeks with three family meetings per week, but may last three months and have somewhat fewer or more than 30 meetings. Each family meeting lasts one hour. This clinical trial targeted arrested youths entering the Hillsborough County Juvenile Assessment Center (Dembo & Brown, 1994) and their families. One year and longer-term outcome studies of the FEI show very promising results (Dembo, Ramirez-Garnica et al., in press and in this volume; Dembo, Seeberger et al., in press a; Dembo, Schmeidler et al., in this volume). This article provides a detailed overview of this innovative, in-home intervention.

Many treatment programs face considerable financial challenges in providing quality services to troubled youths and their families–which often preclude the extensive use of professional therapists. For example, while MST has been found to be effective with noninstitutionalized offenders, this family service tends to be costly (approximately $6,000 per family) because trained therapists usually provide the intervention. Other effective, but more economical, family intervention services are needed to meet the needs of jurisdictions which lack the resources to implement MST. A key feature of the FEI is that intervention services are delivered by Field Consultants, trained paraprofessional staff who are guided by and work under the direction of licensed clinicians. In the YSP, this intervention costs less than $1,500 per family.

THEORETICAL FOUNDATIONS OF THE FEI

The FEI is an in-home program for delinquent youths and their families. It offers highly interactive, experiential activities which facilitate a positive emotional climate, revitalize a family's natural strengths, and improve interpersonal skills. In addition, many of these interventions and activities facilitate a more effective, adaptive, and workable family structure. The FEI is informed by four theoretical approaches: systemic, structural, transgenerational, and psycho-educational.

Systemic

According to a systems approach, family members are interconnected and interdependent of a larger system. Their thoughts, beliefs, and behaviors can be understood as part of an interactive pattern, with each member influencing, evoking, and/or responding to someone else (Bateson, 1979; Bateson, Jackson, Haley, & Weakland, 1956). The interactive patterns of behavior are viewed as predictable, cyclical, and self-sustaining. They are repetitive actions which maintain a familiar and emotionally safe way of operating.

The systemic perspective does not view one family member as having "the problem." Rather, the problem is understood as emerging from the "social field" (Hoffman, 1981) in which it occurs (Haley, 1976). It shows something about the larger picture in the family. Focusing on the social unit, the interactive pattern in the family rather than the individual, can move families away from blaming, scapegoating, or looking for a simple cause. It also raises different, more interesting concerns: What influences do family members have over each other through behaviors, conversations, and nonverbal exchanges? How do family members regulate closeness and distance? How are anger, disagreement, and conflict managed? How are rules and roles established and maintained? In what ways is the family impacted by social forces (schools, social service agencies, law enforcement, media)? What are the historic family legacies, rituals, and myths that influence current family interactions? Questions such as these help identify the depth and complexity of everyday family life.

Structural

The structural approach emphasizes family organization and interactive processes as key concepts in understanding a family (Minuchin, 1974, 1981, 1984). Family dysfunction is understood as a reflection of difficulties in those areas. The central elements of the structural perspective are:

a. *Hierarchy* denotes the organization of power in the family. Who makes the decisions about finances? Household chores? Curfews? Who do the children go to for permission to sleep at a friend's house? How is discipline and limit-setting managed in the family? In well-functioning families, the adult care givers are considered the "executive branch" and have the mechanisms by which to hold appropriate power. Troubled families are characterized by inconsistent, chaotic, and unpredictable organization. Moreover, in those families, the children exert more power than is appropriate. For example, a 12- year-old son who has been "parentified" by his single parent is required to act as a co-parent to a younger sibling.

b. *Subsystems* are smaller units within a family system. These units are well-defined and have their own specific roles and functions (i.e., parent subsystem and sibling subsystem).

c. *Boundaries* are the invisible lines between family members, subsystems, and the larger community. Boundaries are defined by implicit and explicit rules and expectations. Examples include such everyday occurrences as knocking on a parent's or sibling's door before entering his or her bedroom, calling home if more than 30 minutes late, or a family rule that children must ask 24 hours in advance for permission to sleep at a friend's house. Healthy boundaries are created in response to the changing developmental needs of family members. Boundaries strongly affect the nature and health of family subsystems. If they are excessively rigid or inflexible, impermeable barriers between members exist. If they are excessively blurred or vague, a lack of clarity is present. Good boundaries foster a healthy balance between self-differentiation and mutuality.

Since healthy boundaries are essential to a well-functioning family hierarchy, FEI interventions and interactions by Field Consultants encourage strengthening the "executive branch" of the family (e.g., addressing the parents as Mr., Ms., or Mrs., unless they request first names, asking "permission" from parents to make a directive or a suggestion to the target youth, and requesting that parents sit together during the meetings). Each of these interventions relays the message to the parent(s): "We respect your position in this family. You are the head(s) of this household." By doing so, the Field Consultant communicates positive regard toward the parent(s) and models this for the children.

d. *Alignments* are the ways in which family members join together or oppose one another.

For example, Mr. Rodriguez would tend to align himself with the target youth, Luisa, when she broke a family rule such as breaking curfew or failing to do chores. He would do so by making excuses for, or ignoring, her behavior. Frequently, the Rodriguez's would argue about "his always taking up for Luisa." The Field Consultant assisted Mr. and Mrs. Rodriguez in presenting a "united front" when their daughter behaved inappropriately. This represented a more constructive and generationally appropriate alignment.

e. A *triangulation* is an alliance within one subsystem which has a negative impact on another member of the family. These alliances are dysfunctional in that they disrupt family organization and create inappropriate boundaries. The Rodriguez family represents a triangulation of an allied father and daughter "against" mother.

Transgenerational

The transgenerational perspective understands the family as being comprised of an entire kinship network of at least three generations. The current family system is profoundly influenced by their history and family legacy. In order to fully understand and appreciate what happens in the family, it is often helpful to understand the generational context. What were the significant issues in previous generations? Alcoholism? Chronic illness? Sudden death of a spouse? How have these life events affected family members? In what ways do unresolved experiences and struggles get passed down to the present generation?

Families can be viewed as repeating themselves over time. What happens in one generation will often get played out in another one. Although there are variations of behaviors and "scripts," the inherent issues and themes remain the same. These themes influence members' actions, expectations, assumptions, and roles within the family. These recurring patterns become "family echoes." Two examples are:

- The target youth, Isaac, was described by his mother as "just like my daddy . . . lazy and without one whit of sense." How do these expectations affect mother's behavior toward Isaac? To what extent is a self-fulfilling prophecy occurring? How has mother's difficult relationship with her own father affected her style of parenting? To what extent do her negative feelings about her dad get expressed through her son?
- During the second meeting, the father informs the Field Consultant that the target youth's mother committed suicide when the youth was three years old "but since Gina (the target youth) was too young to remember her mother, it has never been discussed." This information can provide the consultant with valuable insight into how this family deals with grief and pain. What other issues are avoided by the family? How does this family manage change and loss? In what ways has Gina dealt with her mother's death?

The Genogram

A genogram is a structured format for drawing a family tree. It records information about family members and structure over a three-generation period. Genograms are usually associated with Bowen's family systems theory (Bowen, 1978; McGoldrick & Gerson, 1985), but are used by a wide range of clinical orientations. A genogram provides a visual picture of the family; it represents the family gestalt. Genograms diagram recurring family difficulties (legal and community involvement, substance abuse, physical or sexual abuse), family strengths and achievements (escaping poverty, graduating high school), historical events (relocations, deaths, long absences), demographics (education, birth dates, presence of chronic illnesses), and predominant familial beliefs, myths, and legacies (e.g., "The Thompson boys have this anger streak. It's just the way we've always been. We don't take any disrespect from anybody").

The Field Consultant constructs the family genogram during the first or second meeting. The reasons for doing so are threefold. First, it offers an excellent opportunity for the Field Consultant to rapidly engage with members in a non-threatening manner. Second, it shifts the focus from the target youth to a family systems perspective. By doing so, family members can "get the big picture" and begin to think differently about their current difficulties. Third, it provides the consultant with valuable information about the family system in a timely manner.

Families often acknowledge that constructing a genogram together provides a rich opportunity to learn about each other's personal stories and shared family history. Genograms are a powerful vehicle to map the evolution of the family and to strengthen bonds between members.

Psycho-Educational

The family's acquisition of successful life management and interpersonal skills is a core objective of the Family Empowerment Intervention. Therefore, the psycho-educational model, which emphasizes skill-building and behavioral change, is used. This model embraces a wide spectrum of approaches which are primarily cognitive-behavioral and instructional. Psycho-educational approaches are used to improve communication, conflict-resolution, anger management, and problem-solving skills. Psycho-educational approaches are also used for developing better social skills at home, school, and in the community. This model emphasizes role playing, homework assignments, and other practical strategies which promote desired behavior change.

FAMILY EMPOWERMENT INTERVENTION GOALS

Deriving from the theoretical foundation of this intervention are its nine specific goals. These goals should be regarded as separate yet interrelated objectives which together strengthen family structure and functioning (Cervenka, Dembo, & Brown, 1996).

1. Restore the family hierarchy (Parents > Children).
2. Restructure boundaries between parents and children.
3. Encourage parents to take greater responsibility for family functioning.
4. Increase family structure through implementation of rules and consequences.
5. Enhance parenting skills.
6. Have parents set limits, expectations, and rules that increase the likelihood that the target youth's behavior will improve.

7. Improve communication skills among all family members and the ability to have fun together.
8. Improve problem-solving skills, particularly in the target youth.
9. Where needed, to connect the family to other systems (school, church, community activities)–"system fit."

STRUCTURAL INTERVENTION STRATEGIES

The Family Empowerment Intervention is described in two complementary documents: (1) a project implementation manual and (2) an activities manual. The *implementation manual* provides the theoretical foundation for the FEI, together with the policies and practices involved in carrying it out. The *activities manual* presents specific games, artistic projects, and exercises in which family members can engage to facilitate achieving the goals of the intervention. The activities manual evolved from our early experience in implementing the FEI, which indicated many of the families we worked with did not respond well to verbal interaction and sharing of feelings and information. The various activities often "bring to light" issues the families are experiencing in a manner which they can directly understand. We have found that project Field Consultants often carry the activities manual with them in the field to plan specific activities for family meetings or to use it in setting up or providing instructions to families involved in specific games, exercises, etc.

The interventions used are primarily strategic in nature. They focus on the here and now with an emphasis on changing repetitive, dysfunctional interactive patterns. The interventions are structured, action-oriented, behavioral, and designed to challenge, shift, interrupt, strengthen, and highlight family processes. Within the context of these interventions, the Field Consultant utilizes six interactional processes: engaging, joining, tracking, enactment, circular questioning, and reframing.

Engaging

Engaging is an interpersonal process whereby the Field Consultant connects with the family in an empathetic and positive manner. This increases the likelihood that the family will accept the Field Consultant and become actively involved with the program. The engagement process is one of the most important aspects of the introduction of the Field Consultant to the family. Successful engagement heightens the family member's sense of being genuinely respected, acknowledged, and understood. This early connection communicates to the family that their involvement in the intervention will be positive and rewarding. The genogram is an excellent vehicle for engaging family members. Using the genogram, the Field Consultant is able to ask everyone questions, facilitate positive conversation, and show interest in the family's history. More importantly, he or she establishes the emotional tone for the helping relationship. The Field Consultant sends the message, "I am interested in your family. I want to know you and it's important that you know one another." For more active, less verbally expressive families, the Field Consultant might postpone using the genogram and bring a puzzle or game. These activities can strengthen the link between the Field Consultant and the more experientially-oriented families. This willingness to engage a family in terms of "where they are at" builds trust and expresses positive regard.

It is important to note that the engagement process continues throughout the intervention. It plays out differently at different times, but its purpose remains the same–to connect with the family in a meaningful way. Although some activities are used for engagement, there is no substitute for an empathetic, present-centered Field Consultant. The quality of "self" is the most important key to successful engagement.

Joining

Joining is another form of engagement with the family; however, it typically denotes a process whereby the Field Consultant specifically connects with one person or subsystem in the family. It is a way of shifting, interrupting, or strengthening an interactional pattern. For instance, the target youth, Elise, is an only child. Frequently, her parents argue about rules and expectations resulting in Elise feeling caught in the middle of a power struggle. As a way of joining, the Field Consultant acknowledges her own experience being the middle child. The Field Consultant may interrupt the parent's arguing by saying to the stepfather, "Boy, I sure remember being caught in the middle of my older brother and younger sister. That wasn't much fun! How do you imagine your stepson might feel right now?" This intervention has three benefits. Firstly, the Field Consultant joins with the target youth by communicating, "Hey, I know how you may feel right now." Secondly, it invites the stepfather to empathize with the target youth. Thirdly, it opens the door for a very different conversation, thereby interrupting the negative, repetitive interactional patterns.

Tracking

Tracking is a strategy whereby the Field Consultant identifies significant and meaningful symbolic expression communicated by family members. For example, in a "family portrait" drawing, a mother drew herself in the corner of the paper. Upon exploration, the mother acknowledged that she frequently felt like going to the corner when family conflict emerged. This metaphor became a meaningful, yet playful, theme which helped this family resolve important issues around anger and conflict. This metaphor enabled the mother to communicate ideas, thoughts, and feelings in a safe, indirect, and creative way. Metaphors offer powerful ways to describe the usual in an unusual manner.

Because many of the activities used in the Family Empowerment Intervention encourage symbolic expression, tracking is a particularly valuable process. It highlights and clarifies the individual language of experience, thus inviting members to gain insight into themselves and other members. Families now have an opportunity to gain a fresh perspective and to develop new ways to respond to one another.

Enactment

Enactment is a process in which family members are instructed to interact in their typical manner and then modify their transactions in more positive ways. For example, Dean, age 13, frequently nags his mother when she sets limits about curfews and friends. After several minutes of this, his father starts to yell at Dean. Name-calling, arguing, and fighting ensues. The enactment is: Step 1: The Field Consultant asks each member to act out their respective, stereotypical part of "the family dance." Step 2: The family is asked to become "observers" of their interaction. What could they have done differently? How could Mom or Dad respond differently? What might be other ways for Dean to deal with his frustration? Step 3: Instruct the family to role play this new interaction. Also, having families review a particular segment of a video recorded at a previous family meeting offers an excellent opportunity for enactment.

Circular Questioning

Based on systems theory, circular questioning is a style of inquiry designed to reveal family patterns and connections. Circular questioning invites family members to reflect on issues, explore individual perceptions, and address concerns in a highly interactive manner. It is based on the view that behaviors are systemic, interactional, repetitive, and predictable. Actions and beliefs of family members are interrelated, each person influencing the other. These interactional patterns are cyclical and exist as feedback loops within the system. We are more accustomed to thinking in linear causality, that one event causes the next in a stimulus-response manner. Hence A would cause B and B would cause C. Circular causality would view each of A, B, and C as causing each other. It suggests that there are forces moving in several directions simultaneously, not simply a single event caused by another.

Circular questioning focuses attention on family connections rather than on individual problems: Who in the family gets most upset? How do other members typically respond to this person? What does Mom do when Dad worries about your sister? What does Susie do when Alex has a tantrum? In what ways does your stepdad show you he really cares about your mother? By asking several family members the same question about a concern, one is able to probe more deeply without being overly confrontational or harsh. The Field Consultant gently "opens the door" to explore the personal meaning of events and relationships within the family. The benefits of circular questioning include: (1) Opening up the family system to new information and understanding of themselves and others. These new perceptions offer members possibilities for innovative and more positive solutions, (2) Increasing empathy, (3) Breaking repetitive, negative interactional patterns, and (4) Communicating to the family that the Field Consultant views each member's perceptions as unique, valuable, and meaningful. By doing so, the Field Consultant strengthens a sense of family empowerment and decreases an overreliance on him or her as the "family expert."

Reframing

Reframing is the technique of relabeling a behavior by putting it into a new, more positive perspective. For example, a stubborn child might be described as focused and persistent. Or a father's criticism of his son might be a sign of the father's best way of expressing his interest and care. Chronic fighting between a mother and daughter is relabeled as an indicator of how "really plugged into one another they must be." Reframing offers members a position of power and competency, rather than deficiency, in dealing with family challenges. The primary objectives of reframing are to: (1) provoke a more positive reaction to the behavior, (2) help individuals view intentions and actions in a fresh way, (3) open up the system to creative change, and (4) show that there is more than one way to see a particular situation.

PHASES OF THE FAMILY EMPOWERMENT INTERVENTION

The Family Empowerment Intervention has been designed to proceed through four phases:

Phase 1. Introductory Phase–First or First/Second Session

Phase 1 is characterized by the introduction of the Field Consultant and all family members involved, a description of the intervention and supervision design, a review of the intervention procedures (including videotaping and audiotaping family meetings) and timing, and responses to any questions the family may have about the YSP.
Content:

> Introduction of everyone present
> Description of the intervention by the Field Consultant
> Introduction of taping program for supervision
> Signatures of all present on taping approval form
> Setup of audio/video
> Presentation of supervision requirement
> Questions posed and answered about the YSP and the FEI
> Introduction of a genogram format
> Construction of the first genogram
> Inquiry as to family style of interacting
> Review of session
> Establishment of at least two additional appointments

Field Consultant is to:

> Use last names for parent generation unless instructed otherwise by them (first session, try to retain formality)
> Have parents introduce children wherever possible
> Observe interaction in response to a new person (Field Consultant)
> Ask what expectations/fears the family members had in letting a new person into their home for many weeks
> Consider feeling tone in the family
> Identify all family members who live in the home
> Try to identify other significant members of the family circle
> Videotape family meetings
> Try, wherever possible, to reframe the focus from the target youth to the whole family (describe FEI as many times as needed)
> Shake everyone's hand, or make close contact with each member, bearing in mind cultural differences in "space" and greeting
> Make eye contact with everyone present at least once
> Keep FEI goals in mind
> Present a positive, hopeful picture to the family before leaving
> Have signed taping form in field notes when leaving

Phase 2. Consultation Phase–Sessions Two/Three through Sessions Nine/Twelve

Phase 2 is characterized by inquiry and participation by the Field Consultant; demonstration methods are used for sharing/asking; Field Consultant conducts activities.

Content:

> Review of prior sessions
>
> Round Robins
>> Family roles and rules
>> Family communication
>> Generational differences and hierarchy
>> Boundaries and relationships
>
> Genogram and family picture construction
>> Discussion of family themes and history
>> Use of paper and pencil, drawings, landscapes with stickers, games, etc., to exemplify family feelings and interactions, "Who in the family . . . " and other tools for family inquiry
>
> Use of communication games, puzzles, etc., to assess family styles and interactions–how can they best work together?
>
> Behavioral methods: positive outcomes, "catch 'em being good," charting
>
> Discussion of discipline, compliance, and consequences
>
> Anger management techniques
>
> Goal setting–individual and family
>
> Review at end of each session; repeat what has occurred
>
> At each session, establishment of at least two additional appointments, repetition of ideal of 3 times per week, 10 weeks

Field Consultant is to:

> Arrange seating by generations for hierarchy establishment
>
> Start with statement about the last session ("I thought about what you said . . . ") and a question about the family's reaction ("What were you thinking about at last time's discussion of . . . ?") to assure continuity and to "link" the sessions in their minds
>
> Keep FEI goals in mind
>
> Start by taking the lead, gradually giving the leadership to the family
>
> Refer to the genogram information at every session
>
> Be sure each person in the family has "air time"

Arrive at each session with a planned agenda of activities
Introduce activities/agendas that include fun/positive feelings
Videotape family meetings
Make eye contact with everyone present at least once
Present a positive, hopeful picture to the family before leaving
Be sure to have agreement as to next meeting time, agenda

Phase 3. Family Work Phase–Sessions Ten/Thirteen to Session 27

Phase 3 is characterized by the family members taking the lead in reorganizing
ways of communicating, relating, thinking about family functioning.
Content:

Workbook activities on behavioral charting, expectations, etc.
Family reviews genograms/family themes together; little
Field Consultant prompting
Family members set personal goals; written statements
where possible
Family sets goals for family as a unit; written statements
where possible
Family decides how to reach new family goals, how to make
life more pleasant and interesting for each other
Family works on issues of roles/responsibilities
Family sets rewards for instances where responsibilities are met
Family sets consequences for failed attempts at being re-
sponsible
Family discusses generational expectations and hierarchy
Family problem solves together
Tasks may be provided by Field Consultant, games, con-
structions, etc.
Family communication is practiced, each with each other in
dyads, triads, generational groups
Target youth describes his/her own brush with the justice
system
Target youth describes plans for constructive activity
Target youth receives support from family for change
Review at end of each session to repeat what has occurred
At each session, establishment of at least two additional
appointments, repetition of ideal of 3 times per week,
10 weeks
Field Consultant is to:
Change seating positions to allow each family member to
communicate naturally with each other

Start with statement about the last session ("I thought about what you said . . . ") and a question about the family's reaction ("What were you thinking about at last time's discussion of . . . ?") to assure continuity and to "link" the sessions in their minds

Have an agenda in mind for each session and those that will follow

Suggest tasks at the beginning of the session, allow family to choose

Be sure the family has the goal areas in mind as they work

Prompt activities when the family gets "stuck"

Provide positive feedback every time initiative is taken by a family member

Model techniques of reflecting, responding, fairness in interaction

Videotape family meetings

Show a videotape from earlier sessions for change recognition

Make eye contact with everyone present at least once

Focus attention upon positive planning for target youth and others

Present a positive, hopeful picture to the family before leaving

Be sure to have agreement as to next meeting time, agenda

Phase 4. Graduation Phase–Final Three Sessions

Phase 4 is characterized by review of the intervention and preparation for separation from the FEI.

Content:

Discussion of change and changes

Overview of goals to be achieved over time

Review of earlier videotapes for confirmation of change

Decision to graduate: family, Field Consultant, consultation with supervisor

Final activities: planning the party

Party and celebration

Field Consultant is to:

Introduce a "future genogram"; where does the family want to be next year, the year after, etc.?

Start with statement about the last session ("I thought about what you said . . .") and a question about the family's reaction ("What were you thinking about last time's discussion of . . . ?") to assure continuity and to "link" the sessions in their minds

Have an agenda for each final session: review, reframe, refresh

Help the family set up methods of communication after the intervention is complete, using the continuity, as above

Review progress made over the course of the intervention

Talk about partings and saying goodbye

Provide positive feedback every time initiative is taken by family member

Model techniques of reflecting, responding, fairness in interaction

Videotape family meetings

Show a videotape from earlier sessions for change recognition

Make eye contact with everyone present at least once

Focus attention upon positive planning for target youth and others

Present a positive, hopeful picture to the family before leaving

Say goodbye to each family member at the party, giving each positive feedback about their role in the project

Remind the family to have fun together before leaving

Present the Certificate of Completion ("diploma")

ENGAGING AND MOVING FAMILIES THROUGH FEI TO GRADUATION

Many of the families with whom we work are difficult to engage. Many of the families who enter our project feel emotionally and economically overwhelmed. They are discouraged and often feel powerless. Many value immediate gratification and do not "buy into" a long-term commitment. Some have long histories of unsatisfying relationships with social service, school, and law enforcement personnel. Other families are highly mobile and often have members living in various residences.

These families can be particularly challenging to work with. Initial involvement in the intervention may be tenuous. Keeping these families connected to the long-term process can be frustrating. We have found the following techniques increase the likelihood of family participation:

1. Involve the families in the intervention quickly. Allow as little time as possible to lapse between acceptance into the intervention and the first meeting.
2. The Field Consultants must be persistent and consistent in their efforts to capture these more challenging families. This may include frequent phone calls, notes on the front door, arriving unexpectedly, or, when appropriate, meeting the target youth at school.
3. Families must be held accountable for the active participation of all members. Field Consultants must send a clear message that "All members play an important role in the family and are expected to be involved in the process."
4. The Field Consultant must be innovative and action-oriented with these particular families. Engagement occurs on an experiential basis rather than an intellectual one; interpersonal connection is made through active involvement. It follows that the particular interventions used should be relevant and enjoyable to the family. The initial activities used should be non-threatening, fun, and meaningful. Moreover, the Field Consultants must communicate hope and the belief that the family's participation will have specific and tangible results.
5. The Field Consultants and clinical staff must view assessment and intervention as an ongoing process. This view requires the intervention team to pay close attention to each family's level of involvement. It demands a flexible, creative, and dynamic orientation to helping families successfully move through each phase of the intervention.

THE ROLE OF THE FIELD CONSULTANT

The primary role of the Field Consultants, under clinical supervision, is to engage in inquiries, tasks, and activities designed to attain the goals and objectives of the Family Empowerment Intervention. To this end, the Field Consultants are to provide direction, constructive feedback and information, and establish a positive "work" atmosphere when meeting with families. Field Consultants are to clarify the goals and objectives of the family and the intervention, review task and homework assignments, and facilitate family members' learning effective life skills. Additionally, Field Consultants act as:

- Role models for good communication, healthy interpersonal boundaries, and leadership. On a more subtle level, Field Consultants model persistence of action, empathy, and optimism.
- Referral sources for "system fits." For example, a Field Consultant may provide information regarding substance abuse counseling services or vocational training for a particular family member.

- Liaison persons between the target youth and other professionals/agencies in the community. When deemed appropriate by the intervention team, the Field Consultant facilitates linking the youth or family with an agency or community resource which can provide a specific service such as job training or mentoring. Since the intervention's objective is family empowerment, primary responsibility for making these links is given to the target youth's caregivers, not the Field Consultant.

For legal and ethical reasons, it is critical that Field Consultants clarify the difference between "consultant" and "therapist" to families. Consultants do not provide psychological treatment services which are beyond the scope of their educational and professional training. Field Consultants do not perform clinical services which are provided by professionals licensed by the State of Florida. This clarification establishes realistic expectations for the family and clarifies the competencies, and limitations, of the Field Consultant.

SELECTING THE FIELD CONSULTANT

The Field Consultants in the YSP held bachelor level degrees in the Social Sciences or Education and had one to two years prior experience working with high-risk youths. The success of the Family Empowerment Intervention primarily depends on the effectiveness of each Field Consultant. This effectiveness is based on several personal and professional competencies. The YSP has identified several personal and professional competencies as critical in being a successful Field Consultant. These competencies include:

Self-Directedness

This position requires a high degree of autonomy, self-organization, and focus. It is crucial that a Field Consultant be internally motivated rather than have a strong need for external structure. The degree of self-directedness is very much associated with the consultant's clear sense of the intervention's goals, vision, and philosophy. It is important that the consultant be effective in setting goals, implementing plans, and following through.

Ability to Tolerate Ambiguity

There are several reasons why it is important that the Field Consultant have a high tolerance for ambiguity. First, many of the families served are highly disorganized and chaotic, which results in unexpected and unpredictable situations at family meetings. Second, Field Consultants often work with families of different ethnic backgrounds, cultural values, and worldviews. These differences require the Field Consultants to suspend judgement and accept individual differences. Third, since the use of games, non-verbal exercises, and other symbolic activities are the cornerstone of the intervention, the helping experiences often occur in a subtle, less obvious manner. This lack of obvious change increases ambiguity and makes it difficult for Field Consultants to see the shifts which are occurring. Lastly, since many aspects of the helping process are intangible and difficult to measure, the Field Consultant must be able to continue his/her efforts with minimal feedback from participants. This lack of feedback can result in feelings of uncertainty and frustration if the Field Consultant is unable to tolerate a certain amount of ambiguity.

It is important to note that one of the many benefits of using videotape in clinical supervision is that it offers visible and concrete feedback to Field Consultants. This feedback lessens the degree of ambiguity which the consultant experiences.

Non-Judgmental and Accepting

The capacity to meaningfully respond to a family in a caring and non-critical manner is essential. Since it is imperative that all families experience a high degree of positive regard by the Field Consultant, an uncritical attitude must be present. This non-judgmental position includes being emotionally supportive and non-blaming toward all who receive this intervention.

Communication Skills

Training must include the development of effective communication skills, which are necessary to be an effective Field Consultant. These skills are primarily active listening, paraphrasing, and the use of open-ended questions. Since the theoretical basis of this intervention is systemic, the Field Consultant must be able to communicate so as to increase meaningful interaction among family members. This circular style of interaction is designed to engage all members and facilitates positive communication within the family. Also, by emphasizing interaction among family members, the Field Consultant increases the family's sense of competency and belief that they can operate in a constructive way.

Empathy

Empathy, the ability to see the world as another does, is a critical aspect of being an effective Field Consultant. The ability to suspend one's own world-view so as to relate to the unique experiences of family members is vital to a successful intervention. This sensitivity is central to responding to family members in a caring and accepting manner.

Although empathy is a highly idiosyncratic trait, the YSP has found that increasing empathy among Field Consultants is facilitated by: (a) frequent and active involvement with families, (b) review of videotaped family visits in supervision, (c) the use of role playing and other experiential activities in training and supervision, and (d) involvement in settings which are familiar to the family (i.e., scheduling a visit with the target youth at school, visiting the community's youth detention center).

An Orientation Toward Action

It is important that the Field Consultant take a highly active role in both the structure and process of the Family Empowerment Intervention. For example, Field Consultants usually need to be persistent and tenacious in scheduling family meetings and set an expectation that all members participate when appropriate. It is vital that Field Consultants hold family members accountable for consistent participation in this intervention. Since successful participation in the Family Empowerment Intervention is based on families engaging in structured activities, moving through phases, and reaching specific goals, it is crucial that Field Consultants provide initiative, direction, and leadership.

Also, since many of the families involved in the juvenile justice system tend to be concrete, rather than abstract, and action-oriented, as opposed to insight-oriented, Field Consultants will more powerfully engage members by the use of action approaches.

Self-Awareness

The role of Field Consultant requires insight, self-understanding, and self-reflection. The degree to which Field Consultants genuinely understand themselves is very much related to their effectiveness with families. This understanding must include familial, social, and emotional forces which have affected their lives. For example, one Field Consultant in the YSP had a consistent pattern of avoiding family conflict by using humor to lessen his own discomfort. Clinical supervision explored how earlier coping styles in his own family influenced his current behavior with families.

Along with self-awareness, it is important for Field Consultants to develop the capacity for self-acceptance and have a commitment to personal growth. Like empathy, self-awareness is a highly idiosyncratic trait; however, there are certain environmental conditions which enhance a Field Consultant's capacity for self-understanding. These conditions are: (a) a trusting, emotionally safe relationship with the supervisory staff, (b) an overall atmosphere of acceptance of, and support for, self-discovery, and (c) the program administration's sensitivity to, and respect for, the unique challenges of this form of field experience.

INITIAL TRAINING OF FIELD CONSULTANTS

Prior to implementing the Family Empowerment Intervention, new Field Consultants undergo a four to six week training period under the coaching and guidance of project clinical staff and other more experienced Field Consultants. During this period: (1) they are provided with the theoretical foundation of the Family Empowerment Intervention; (2) they learn the policies and procedures involved, and the various activities used, in the intervention–as well as various community resources; and (3) they shadow more experienced Field Consultants with active family caseloads.

When clinical staff feel the trainee is ready, he/she is assigned a family to work with. Here, again, the Field Consultant receives coaching and guidance from his/her clinical supervisor. Videotapes of family meetings are a major tool for improving technique. As the Field Consultant's clinical supervisor gains confidence in his/her ability to implement the Family Empowerment Intervention, the consultant's caseload is increased until a full caseload is reached. After the introductory and transition periods, Field Consultants are expected to handle six family cases simultaneously.

ENSURING THE INTEGRITY OF INTERVENTION SERVICES

It is essential to adequately train Field Consultants to implement high quality intervention services and to ensure that these services remain at high quality. The maintenance of quality services is an ongoing process including the following elements:

1. Field Consultant Weekly Meetings with Clinical Supervisors (discussed in more detail below): Field Consultants meet with their clinical supervisors once a week for 1 1/2 hours to review their families' cases and to receive guidance on strategies and activities to use in helping families reach the intervention's goals.
2. Bi-Weekly Group Supervision Meetings (discussed in more detail below): During these meetings, Field Consultants show videotapes of

family meetings to the other Field Consultants and clinical staff, and receive ideas and coaching on how to work more effectively with them.

3. Weekly Field Consultant Training Sessions: Each week, Field Consultants receive 1 1/2 hours of training on various topics relating to the intervention: for example, its theoretical foundation, the connection between specific goals of the intervention and activities used in working with families, new community agencies/services and the procedures to use for "system fits."

4. Bi-Weekly Clinical Staff and Project Director Meetings: At these meetings, the project director, and clinical staff (line clinical supervisors and clinical coordinator) discuss administrative issues affecting service delivery (e.g., coordination with other agencies supervising the target youth) and project service delivery integrity issues (e.g., training topics); and steps are taken to resolve these issues.

5. Weekly Project Meetings: Each week, Field Consultants, clinical staff, and administrative staff (i.e., the project director and administrative assistant coordinator) meet to discuss any issues affecting the delivery of quality services (e.g., caseload size), share information (e.g., identifying new community services), review family enrollment into the intervention, and reaffirm commitment to our common purpose.

Clinical Supervision

The clinical supervisor-Field Consultant relationship is a critical factor in the effectiveness of intervention services. Since the intervention utilizes BA level paraprofessionals, the need for a consistent, emotionally supportive supervisory relationship is an essential ingredient for success. Individual supervision is held weekly, 1 1/2 hours per Field Consultant.

The role and function of the supervisor are multidimensional; the supervisor provides technical expertise, emotional support, administrative assistance, mentoring, and clinical training and education. The YSP has identified a number of key elements of the effective supervisor-Field Consultant process:

- To provide specific and concrete instruction to Field Consultants; an emphasis on skill-building in the areas of family systems theory, structural and strategic intervention, life-skills (e.g, communication, conflict-resolution, anger management), and interpersonal relations. The use of video and audiotaped family meetings is an integral component to successful instruction.
- To provide direction and encouragement to the Field Consultant about further training and educational opportunities (e.g., local workshops, relevant books and journals, university course work).

- To teach and model effective clinical skills including empathy, positive regard, acceptance, as well as specific family systems techniques and interventions.
- To instruct Field Consultants in the theory and use of the games and activities.
- To assist in decisions about phase determination for a particular family. To what degree is the family meeting their own and the intervention's goals? What impasses are the family members, target youth, or Field Consultant experiencing? What activities or interventions might support positive change for the family? How can these changes most effectively be monitored?
- To assist Field Consultants' working through their own personal issues. As in any helping relationship, the caregiver's insight and self-awareness are key in maintaining healthy interpersonal boundaries, establishing clear goals, and self-calibration. The supervisor is instrumental in facilitating increased self-understanding by the Field Consultant. The supervisory relationship offers a supportive atmosphere for Field Consultants to understand the impact of their own family system, gain greater sensitivity to cultural influences and assumptions, and develop a better understanding of, and for, their emotional world.
- To provide emotional and professional support to Field Consultants. This support includes sharing clinical feedback, encouragement, and technical skills which increase the Field Consultants' level of expertise and confidence.
- To be a "sounding board" for the Field Consultants; to facilitate creative problem-solving, innovative use of existing interventions and activities, and to brainstorm ideas and strategies with which to foster positive change within a family.
- To help organize daily and weekly activities of the Field Consultant.
- To reinforce the intervention's goals, theoretical orientation, and vision.

Group Supervision

Along with individual supervision, group supervision meetings are held on a biweekly basis for two hours. These meetings are comprised of all Field Consultants, clinical supervisors, the clinical director, and project director. Group supervision offers instruction and case supervision using the video or audiotapes made by the Field Consultants during family meetings. Usually, the Field Consultants bring one or two tapes to be reviewed and discussed by all staff. The focus of discussion is primarily on:

- Feedback regarding family process, dynamics, and interaction.
- Feedback on the responses and specific interventions of the Field Consultant.
- Review of goals and objectives of the intervention as they relate to the particular family.
- Development of clinical hypotheses and interventions.

Along with providing training and education, group supervision offers an invaluable opportunity for professional support for Field Consultants. The group supervisory process provides a supportive environment in which to share ideas and feelings, examine specific challenges, and increase self-understanding. In doing so, the work of all staff improves and relationships become strengthened. The benefits of group supervision also include: (1) receiving peer support and technical assistance, (2) strengthening a sense of bondedness and professional support, (3) developing a shared connection thereby decreasing professional isolation, and (4) acquiring understanding and skills through vicarious learning.

Field Consultant In-Service Training

Ongoing training for Field Consultants is a critical aspect of the YSP. Training is provided for 1 1/2 hours on a weekly basis by one of the clinical staff. In general, all training has a strong experiential component, enhancing both the conceptual and practical dimensions of the learning experience. In addition, Field Consultants have many opportunities for training off-site, and receive in-service programs from other professionals in the community. *It is critical that a continual linkage be maintained between these activities and exercises and the goals of the intervention so that treatment integrity is sustained.*

There are three major content areas of training:

1. *The use and refinement of the family activities.* Although it is important for the Field Consultants to have a theoretical understanding of the family activities, great emphasis is placed on "hands-on" experience. The benefits of this experiential approach are twofold; Field Consultants: (1) learn how to effectively use these creative and innovative approaches through behavioral rehearsal, and (2) increase empathy for the families with whom they work. Additionally, these sessions provide opportunities to role-play specific challenges presented by a particular family. This training is an excellent vehicle for

sharing constructive feedback, modifying, updating, and fine-tuning materials, and developing new materials for families.

2. *General topics in the helping process.* The YSP provided training in a wide range of topics, including systems theory, structural and strategic interventions, family and human development, and life management skills. Examples of some areas of concentration are:

- Systems Theory: information on family organization, boundaries, hierarchies, communications processes, alliances and power issues; the impact of the wider culture on the family; the family as a dynamic system which impacts, and is impacted by, its members; the clinical use and meaning of the genogram.
- Family and Human Development: individual and family development from a life-cycle perspective; normative psychosocial developmental tasks of childhood, adolescence, and adulthood; gender and ethnicity within the family context.
- Life Management: Effective communication skills for all family members; the development of conflict-resolution, negotiation, and anger management strategies; goal-setting, problem-solving, and time- management skills.

3. *The unique issues affecting "at-risk" youths.* The following topics are covered: issues in addiction; at-risk, resiliency, and cultural diversity issues for children and teens; depression and suicide; violence prevention; sexuality and teen pregnancy; the juvenile justice system; community resources and referral.

CRISIS INTERVENTION

Field Consultants are trained to identify and respond to family crises particularly in the areas of child abuse, homicidal or suicidal threats, drug or alcohol related crises, and severe psychological conditions. Where possible, highest priority emergency response by community crisis teams should be established for all families enrolled in the intervention.

The following subsections describe the crisis intervention procedures the YSP established for the Family Empowerment Intervention project in Tampa, Florida. They should be regarded as examples of procedures which can be established and implemented in other communities.

Alcohol and Other Drug Abuse

Youth needing detoxification and stabilization services for substance abuse can be referred to the Agency for Community Treatment Services

(ACTS) Addiction Receiving Facility, located on the ground floor of the Juvenile Assessment Center building. This short-term program, which evaluates and refers youths needing additional services to specific agencies, is open 24 hours a day, seven days a week. A number of community substance abuse treatment programs also exist to treat adults.

Child Abuse or Neglect

By law, professionals working with children are required to report cases of suspected child abuse or neglect to the Florida Department of Child and Family services. The phone number is 1-800-96-ABUSE. For parents/guardians who appear at risk of harming their children, the following resources are available to Field Consultants: in Tampa, the Child Abuse Council; two national help lines are also available: 1-800-FLA-LOVE (available 24 hours) and 1-800-FOR-A-CHILD.

Suicidal Thoughts and Behavior and Other Mental Health Issues

Suicide and other mental health issues also deserve quick and effective responses. Arrangements were made with the Baylife Acute Care Center, Mobile Crisis Response Team, to provide crisis intervention and psychiatric services for the YSP. These services were available for youths, siblings, and their parents/guardians.

Duty to Warn

Following the Tarasoff case in California, therapists having reason to believe a client is likely to harm another person are required to take steps to protect that other person from being hurt. Our staff of Field Consultants is also under obligation to warn those to whom a threat has been made.

Reporting Injuries and Incidents

During the course of their work, Field Consultants may receive injuries or experience incidents involving clients or their families (e.g., client threats). These injuries or experiences should be recorded, and the forms recording these events should be placed in the project files. Consistent with YSP policy, an injury report or incident report (or both if needed) needs to be completed and submitted to the project director for review and follow-up action.

STAFF AND FAMILY SAFETY ISSUES

Since intervention services take place in the field, considerable attention should be given to developing and maintaining Field Consultant and family safety procedures.

Field Consultants

Field Consultants going into the field should sign out on a control board at the unit's office. Sign out and projected return times should be monitored, and steps should be taken to contact staff who are in the field but not heard from for longer than reasonably expected periods of time. Field Consultants should also carry beepers, so that headquarters staff can page them for a check-in call. Further, Field Consultants should carry mobile phones and should be expected to maintain contact with project headquarters. Any requests for information, support or assistance should be responded to immediately.

In situations which appear to have safety concerns, it is strongly recommended that Field Consultants be accompanied by other staff on visits to families. If the homes themselves are unsafe, then arrangements should be made for family meetings to be held in local neighborhood centers such as churches, day care centers, or community service centers.

Project Youth and Their Families

The protection of Family Empowerment Intervention clients and their families is also of concern. Field Consultants should take every reasonable precaution to protect the safety and security of youths and families involved in the intervention.

CONCLUSION

The Family Empowerment Intervention represents an exciting opportunity to intervene effectively in the lives of juvenile offenders and their families. The intervention seeks to strengthen the most significant determinant of favorable long-term outcomes for children: improving the family's own functioning and ability to find effective solutions for their problems. By intervening in the family system, the Field Consultant effects change in the family's interactions in more healthy and appropriate directions. These changes in family functioning can be expected to result in more prosocial changes in the target youth's behavior. Short-term and long-term follow-up results suggest that the Family Empowerment Intervention can reduce the probability that juvenile offenders will continue criminal and high health-risk behavior into adulthood (Dembo, Ramirez-Garnica et al., in press and in this volume; Dembo, Seeberger et al., in press; Dembo, Schmeidler et al., in this volume).

The Family Empowerment Intervention addresses creatively the issues of treatment entry and retention, which, as described earlier, present considerable challenges in treating drug abusing adolescents (Battjes, Onken, & Delany, 1999). The intervention also responds effectively to the need for innovative services for minority and inner city youths and their families, who have historically been underserved (Arcia, Keyes, Gallagher et al., 1993; Dembo & Seeberger, 1999). When seeking publicly funded services, they are often required to visit program offices at some distance from their homes. Providing in-home care by culturally sensitive staff can help eliminate barriers to treatment and permit the FEI to meet families on their own terms.

REFERENCES

Alexander, J.F., & Parsons, B.V. (1982). *Functional Family Therapy: Principles and Procedures.* Carmel, CA: Brooks/Cole.

Anglin, M.D., & Speckart, G. (1988). Narcotics use and crime: A multisample, multimethod analysis. *Criminology, 26,* 197-233.

Arcia, E., Keyes, L., Gallagher, J.J., & Herrick, H. (1993). National portrait of sociodemographic factors associated with underutilization of services: Relevance to early intervention. *Journal of Early Intervention, 17,* 283-297.

Armstrong, T.L., & Altschuler, D.M. (1998). Recent developments in juvenile aftercare: Assessment, findings, and promising programs. In Albert R. Roberts (Ed.), *Juvenile Justice.* 2nd ed. Chicago: Nelson-Hall.

Bateson, G. (1979). *Mind and Nature.* New York: E.P. Dutton.

Bateson, G., Jackson, D., Haley, J., & Weakland, J. (1956). Toward a theory of schizophrenia. *Behavioral Science, 1,* 251-264.

Battjes, R.J., Onken, L.S., & Delany, P.J. (1999). Drug abuse treatment entry and engagement: Report of a meeting on treatment readiness. *Journal of Clinical Psychology, 55,* 643-657.

Bowen, M. (1978). *Family Therapy in Clinical Practice.* New York: Jason Aronson.

Butts, J.A., & Harrell, A.V. (1998). *Delinquents or Criminals: Policy Options for Young Offenders.* Washington, DC: The Urban League.

Catalano, R.F., Hawkins, J.D., Wells, E.A., Miller, J., & Brewer, D. (1990-1991). Evaluation of the effectiveness of adolescent drug abuse treatment, assessment of risks for relapse, and promising approaches for relapse prevention. *The International Journal of the Addictions, 25,* 1085-1140.

Cervenka, K.A., Dembo, R., & Brown, C.H. (1996). A family empowerment intervention for families of juvenile offenders. *Aggression and Violent Behavior: A Review Journal, 1,* 205-216.

Dembo, R., & Brown, R. (1994). The Hillsborough County Juvenile Assessment Center. *Journal of Child and Adolescent Substance Abuse, 3,* 25-43.

Dembo, R., Ramirez-Garnica, G., Rollie, M., Schmeidler, J., Livingston, S., & Hartsfield, A. (In press). Youth recidivism 12 months after a Family Empowerment Intervention: Final report. *Journal of Offender Rehabilitation.*

Dembo, R., Ramirez-Garnica, G., Schmeidler, J., Rollie, M., Livingston, S., & Hartsfield, A. (2001). Long-term impact of a Family Empowerment Intervention on juvenile offender recidivism. *Journal of Offender Rehabilitation, 33:1,* 33-57.

Dembo, R., Schmeidler, J., Nini-Gough, B., & Manning, D. (1998). Sociodemographic, delinquency-abuse history, and psychosocial functioning differences among juvenile offenders of various ages. *Journal of Child and Adolescent Substance Abuse, 8,* 63-78.

Dembo, R., & Seeberger, W. (April 1999). The Need for Innovative Approaches to Meet the Substance Abuse and Mental Health Service Needs of Inner-City, African-American Male Youth Involved with the Juvenile Justice System. Presented before the U.S. Commission on Civil Rights, Washington, DC.

Dembo, R., Seeberger, W., Shemwell, M., Schmeidler, J., Klein, L., Rollie, M., Pacheco, K., Hartsfield, A., & Wothke, W. (in press). Psychosocial functioning among juvenile offenders 12 months after Family Empowerment Intervention. *Journal of Offender Rehabilitation.*

Dembo, R., Schmeidler, J., Seeberger, W., Shemwell, M., Rollie, M., Pacheco, K., Livingston, S., & Wothke, W. (2001). Long-term impact of a Family Empowerment Intervention on juvenile offender psychosocial functioning. *Journal of Offender Rehabilitation, 33:1,* 59-109.

Dembo, R., Williams, L., & Schmeidler, J. (1998). Key findings from the Tampa longitudinal study of juvenile detainees: Contributions to a theory of drug use and delinquency among high risk youths. In Albert R. Roberts (Ed.), *Juvenile Justice.* 2nd ed. Chicago: Nelson-Hall.

Dembo, R., Williams, L., Wothke, W., Schmeidler, J., & Brown, C.H. (1992). The role of family factors, physical abuse and sexual victimization experiences in high risk youths' alcohol and other drug use and delinquency: A longitudinal model. *Violence and Victims, 7,* 245-266.

Grant, B. (2000). Estimates of US children exposed to alcohol abuse and dependence in the family. *American Journal of Public Health, 90:1,* 113-115.

Haley, J. (1976). *Problem Solving Therapy.* San Francisco, CA: Jossey-Bass.

Henggeler, S.W. (1997). The development of effective drug-abuse services for youth. In J.A. Egertson, D.M. Fox, & A.I. Leshner (Eds.), *Treating Drug Abuse Effectively.* Williston, VT: Blackwell Publishers.

Henggeler, S.W., Pickrel, S.G., Brondino, M.J., & Crouch, J.L. (1996). Eliminating (almost) treatment dropout of substance abusing or dependent delinquents through home-based multisystemic therapy. *American Journal of Psychiatry, 153,* 427-428.

Henggeler, S.W., Schoenwald, S.K., Pickrel, S.G., Brondino, M.J., Borduin, C.M., & Hall, J.A. (1994). *Treatment Manual for Family Preservation Using Multisystemic Therapy.* South Carolina Health and Human Services Finance Commission.

Hoffman, L. (1981). *Foundations of Family Therapy: A Conceptual Framework for Systems Change.* New York: Basic Books.

Institute for Health Policy (1993). *Substance Abuse: The Nation's Number One Health Problem.* Waltham, MA: Institute for Health Policy.

Klitzner, M., Fisher, D., Stewart, K., & Gilbert, S. (1991). *Report to the Robert Wood Johnson Foundation on Strategies for Early Intervention with Children and Youth to Avoid Abuse of Addictive Substances.* Bethesda, MD: Pacific Institute for Research and Evaluation.

Kumpfer, K. & Alvarado, R. (1998). *Effective Family Strengthening Interventions.* Washington, DC: U.S. Department of Justice.

McGoldrick, M., & Gerson, R. (1985). *Genograms in Family Assessment*. New York: W.W. Norton & Company.

Minuchin, S. (1974). *Families and Family Therapy*. Cambridge, MA: Harvard University Press.

Minuchin, S. (1981). *Family Therapy Techniques*. Cambridge, MA: Harvard University Press.

Minuchin, S. (1984). *Family Kaleidoscope*. Cambridge, MA: Harvard University Press.

National Institute of Justice (1999). *1998 Annual Report on Drug Use Among Adult and Juvenile Arrestees*. Washington, DC: U.S. Department of Justice.

Office of National Drug Control Policy (1997). *What America's Users Spend on Illegal Drugs, 1988-1995*. (Prepared by Rhodes, W., Langenbahn, S., Kling, R., & Sherman, P.) Washington, DC: ONDCP.

Rahdert, E., & Czechowicz, D. (Eds.) (1995). *Adolescent Drug Abuse: Clinical Assessment and Therapeutic Interventions*. Rockville, MD: National Institute on Drug Abuse.

Snyder, H., & Sickmund, M. (1995). *Juvenile Offenders and Victims: A National Report*. Washington, DC: Office of Juvenile Justice and Delinquency Prevention.

Winters, K.C. (1998). Substance Abuse and Juvenile Offenders. University of Minnesota. Presentation at Physicians Leadership for National Drug Policy Conference. Washington, DC 11-6-98.

AUTHORS' NOTES

Richard Dembo, PhD, is a professor of Criminology at the University of South Florida in Tampa. He has a long-term interest in developing, implementing, and evaluating intervention programs for high-risk youths.

Gary DuDell, PhD, is a licensed therapist and adjunct professor in the University of South Florida, Department of Rehabilitation and Mental Health Counseling. He was a key clinical staff member of the Youth Support Project, providing clinical supervision and training, among other services, to the project.

Stephen Livingston, BA, is a research assistant in the Department of Criminology at the University of South Florida. He has been associated with the Youth Support Project since 1998.

James Schmeidler, PhD, is an assistant professor in the Department of Psychiatry and Biomathematical Sciences at the Mt. Sinai School of Medicine. He has considerable experience applying statistical procedures to behavioral science data.

The preparation of this manuscript was supported by Grant #1-RO1-DA08707, funded by the National Institute on Drug Abuse. The authors are grateful for their support. However, the research results reported and the views expressed in the article do not necessarily imply any policy or research endorsement by our funding agency.

The authors would like to thank clinical, intervention, and other research staff for their contributions to this project. Great thanks are due to project Field Consultants for their work. The authors deeply appreciate the support of Mr. Darrell Manning, supervisor of the Juvenile Assessment Center; he was a great resource to the work.

Address correspondence to Richard Dembo, PhD, Criminology Department, University of South Florida, 4202 E. Fowler Avenue, Tampa, FL 33620.

Family Empowerment as an Intervention Strategy in Juvenile Delinquency. Pp. 33-57.

Long-Term Impact
of a Family Empowerment Intervention
on Juvenile Offender Recidivism

RICHARD DEMBO

Department of Criminology, University of South Florida, Tampa

GABRIELA RAMIREZ-GARNICA

Department of Epidemiology and Biostatistics, University of South Florida, Tampa

JAMES SCHMEIDLER

Departments of Psychiatry and Biomathematical Sciences, Mt. Sinai School of Medicine, New York

MATTHEW ROLLIE

Department of Environmental and Occupational Health, University of South Florida, Tampa

STEPHEN LIVINGSTON

Department of Criminology, University of South Florida, Tampa

AMY HARTSFIELD

Department of Criminology, University of South Florida, Tampa

ABSTRACT We report the results of a study of the long-term impact of a Family Empowerment Intervention (FEI) on recidivism among all 303 youths processed at the Hillsborough County Juvenile Assessment Center who entered the project. The FEI seeks to improve family functioning by empowering parents. Families involved in the project were randomly assigned to either receive an Extended Services Intervention (ESI) or the FEI. Families in the ESI group received monthly phone contacts and, if indicated, referral information; FEI families received three one-hour, home-based meetings per week over a 10-week period from a clinician-trained paraprofessional. The results provide support for the sustained effect of FEI services in reducing recidivism. Analysis indicated that youths who completed the FEI experienced marginally statistically significant, lower rates of new charges and new arrests than youths who did not complete the FEI. The results add to the findings of our earlier 12-month recidivism analyses, which provided strong evidence of the deterrence effects of the FEI. *[Article copies available for a fee from The Haworth Document Delivery Service: 1-800-342-9678. E-mail address: <getinfo@haworthpressinc.com> Website: <http://www.HaworthPress.com> © 2001 by The Haworth Press, Inc. All rights reserved.]*

KEYWORDS Juvenile offender recidivism, juvenile offender family intervention and long-term recidivism, impact of Family Empowerment Intervention on juvenile offender recidivism

INTRODUCTION

Implementing effective intervention programs to address the multiple problems often experienced by youths entering the juvenile justice system, and their families, remains a critical need (Sherman et al., 1997). Innovative service delivery strategies continue to be especially needed for minority and inner-city youths and families who have been underserved in regard to their mental health and substance misuse service needs (Arcia, Keyes, Gallagher, & Herrick, 1993; Sirles, 1990; Tolan, Ryan, & Jaffe, 1988). In the absence of effective intervention services, all too many youths entering the juvenile justice system will, as they grow older, move to the adult justice system and consume a large and growing amount of local, state, and national criminal justice and mental health resources (Office of National Drug Control Policy, 1997). Early intervention holds promise of cost-effectively reducing the probability that troubled youths will continue criminal and high health-risk behavior into adulthood (Klitzner, Fisher, Stewart, & Gilbert, 1991).

Research has consistently documented that many youths entering the juvenile justice system are experiencing multiple personal, educational, and family problems (Dembo, Turner, Schmeidler, Chin Sue, Borden, & Manning, 1996). Among the problems most consistently reported by researchers are: *physical abuse* (Dembo, Williams, & Schmeidler, 1998), *sexual victimization* (Dembo, Williams, & Schmeidler, 1998; Dembo, Wothke, Shemwell, Pacheco, Seeberger, Rollie, & Schmeidler, in press), *poor emotional/psychological functioning* (Teplin & Swartz, 1989; Dembo, Williams, Berry, Getreu, Washburn, Wish, & Schmeidler, 1990), *poor educational functioning* (Dembo, Williams, Schmeidler, & Howitt, 1991) and *alcohol and other drug use* (Dembo, Pacheco, Schmeidler, Fisher, & Cooper, 1997). Many of these youths' difficulties can be traced to *family alcohol/other drug use, mental health, or crime problems* which began when they were young (Dembo, Wothke et al., in press; Dembo, Williams, Wothke, Schmeidler, & Brown, 1992). The interrelationship of these problems urges that holistic, not one problem at a time, services be developed for these youths and their families. Unfortunately, juvenile justice agencies in most jurisdictions have limited resources for providing treatment, and many youths entering the juvenile justice system come from families lacking resources to pay for care. Innovative, low cost, effective efforts continue to be critically needed in which staff working with delinquent youths and their families are trained to provide in-home intervention services (to increase family participation) and, where indicated, to link them with other community resources. As the University of Colorado Center for the Study and Prevention of Violence (1999) asserts, it is important that these intervention programs have been proven effective by evaluation studies reflecting a strong research design, providing strong evidence of prevention or deterrence effects, documenting sustained effects, and indicating multi-site replication.

Such programs hold promise of improving services available to various high-risk youths and their families, especially to African-American and Latino families, who have traditionally had lower service utilization rates for substance misuse and mental health treatment, than Anglo families. Minority and inner-city youths are often socialized in communities and families that are economically and socially stressed. The psychosocial strain experienced by these youths increases their risk of future drug use and delinquency/crime (Nurco, Balter & Kinlock, 1994) and impedes their development as socially responsible and productive adults (Le Blanc, 1990).

A number of intervention efforts, focusing on family preservation and informed by an ecological systems view (Bronfenbrenner, 1979), are being implemented in various parts of the U.S. (e.g., Rahdert & Czechowicz, 1995; Kumpfer & Alvarado, 1998; Szapocznik & Kurtines, 1989). For example, multisystemic therapy (MST) has been found successful in addressing the needs of juvenile offenders and their families (Henggeler & Borduin, 1990; Henggeler, Melton, Smith, Schoenwald, & Hanley, 1993; Henggeler, Schoenwald, Pickrel, Brondino, Borduin, & Hall, 1994). Clinical trials of MST have involved service delivery at community mental health centers. Trained therapists have provided services to four to six "at-risk youths" and their families for as long as four to five months. The family preservation focus of MST seeks to "empower parents to restructure their environments in ways that promote development" (Henggeler, Schoenwald, Pickrel, Brondino, Borduin, & Hall, 1994, p. 21) by developing their parental competencies. From a structural family therapy perspective, an essential first step is to focus on the parents in order to restructure the family and establish parental control. A second goal is to teach the parents how to use agencies and services, including schools, more effectively (Henggeler et al., 1994).

Functional family therapy (Alexander & Parsons, 1982) has been found effective in treating youths 11 to 18 years of age who are involved in alcohol or other drug abuse or delinquent behavior, and in reducing justice and other service system costs in serving these youths. A wide range of trained interventionists, working in one or two person teams, provide from eight to 26 hours of in-home services, involving five phases (engagement, motivation, assessment, behavior change, and generalization) to referred youths and their families.

Another innovative intervention was employed by the Youth Support Project (YSP) in Tampa, Florida. The goal of the project's Family Empowerment Intervention (FEI) is to improve family functioning through empowering parents. As discussed in more detail in the next section, YSP services were provided by trained paraprofessional staff working under the guidance of licensed clinicians.

In a 12-month recidivism study, strong evidence was obtained regarding a beneficial one-year outcome effect of FEI services on youths who completed the intervention. FEI completers experienced significantly lower rates of new charges and significantly fewer new arrests, than youths not completing the FEI (Dembo, Ramirez-Garnica, Rollie, Schmeidler, Livingston, & Hartsfield, in press). Although these recidivism analyses provided convincing evidence of the intervention's effectiveness in reducing 12-month recidivism, it is equally important to assess any *sustained effects* the FEI has on recidivism. Intervention programs can often demonstrate success in reducing recidivism while youths are involved in the program or for a short period afterwards. Substantially fewer programs can document continued beneficial effects for periods longer than one-year post-intervention (University of Colorado Center for the Study and Prevention of Violence, 1999). Depending on the year in which a youth entered the project, we tracked recidivism from 12 months up to 48 months following random assignment to the 10-week intervention. The results of the long-term recidivism analyses describe the *sustained effect* of the FEI on recidivism.

METHOD

The Youth Support Project

As discussed in more detail elsewhere, the YSP implemented a systems-oriented approach to family preservation: a home-based Family Empowerment Intervention (FEI) (Cervenka, Dembo, & Brown, 1996; Dembo, Shemwell, Guida, Schmeidler, Pacheco, & Seeberger, 1998). This innovative experimental, prospective longitudinal study involved up to four interview data collection waves and recidivism analyses. Families involved in the project were randomly assigned into one of two groups: the Extended Services Intervention (ESI) or the Family Empowerment Intervention (FEI) group. ESI group families received monthly phone contacts from project Research Assistants (RAs) and, if indicated, referral information; FEI group families received personal in-home services from project Field Consultants (FCs). Project FCs visit families to work on the following goals: (1) to restore the family hierarchy (parents, children, etc.); (2) to restructure boundaries between parents and children; (3) to encourage parents to take greater responsibility for family functioning; (4) to increase family structure through implementation of rules and consequences; (5) to enhance parenting skills; (6) to have parents set limits, expectations, and rules that increase the likelihood that the target youth's behavior will improve; (7) to improve communication skills among all family members; (8) to improve problem-solving skills, particularly in the target youth; and (9) where needed, to connect the family to other systems (e.g., school, church, community activities). The major hypothesis of the project was that empowering parents will reduce target youth recidivism and increase target youth prosocial behavior and psychosocial functioning.

FEI families were expected to participate in three, one-hour family meetings per week for approximately ten weeks. All household members (i.e., persons living under the same roof as the target youth) were expected to participate in these meetings. Both FEI and ESI families had 24-hour a day, seven days a week access to YSP staff, and to information on various community resources via a project developed agency and services resource file. YSP staff provided families with information about different community agencies and assisted them in obtaining appropriate referrals to meet their needs.

A distinctive feature of this intervention is that the families were served by Field Consultants, who are not trained therapists–although they are trained by, and performed their work under the direction of, licensed clinicians. The choice of paraprofessionals was based on a cost effectiveness argument. Experimental research indicates that, at least for some treatments, paraprofessionals produce outcomes that are better than those under control conditions, and similar to those involving professional therapists (Christensen & Jacobson, 1994; Weisz, Weiss, Han, Granger, & Morton, 1995). By requiring less previous therapy training, the FEI is more likely to be funded, given the increased financial limitations now facing agencies which provide services to juvenile offenders.

Sampling

Youths processed at the Hillsborough County Juvenile Assessment Center (JAC) (Dembo & Brown, 1994) who were arrested on misdemeanor or felony charges were sampled for inclusion in the project. When openings occurred on the Field Consultants' case loads, a listing of recently arrested youths was drawn. A cross-tabulation of these cases was completed in regard to their gender and a variable reflecting race/ethnicity (Hispanic [Latino], Black, non-Hispanic [African-American], and White, non-Hispanic [Anglo]), and equal numbers of youths in each of these six cells were randomly selected for enrollment in the Youth Support Project. This procedure and large sample size provided good representation of African-American, Latino, and Anglo youths of both sexes and their families and improved statistical power for these group comparisons. The data reported in this article include all 303 youths entering the YSP during the period September 1, 1994 to December 31, 1997.

Data Collection

Each youth completed an initial in-depth assessment, for which $10.00 was paid, prior to being randomly assigned to the FEI or ESI group. This included demographics, education, treatment history, family problems, friends' substance abuse, sexual victimization, alcohol and illicit drug use, delinquent behavior, and emotional/psychological functioning. Official record information was obtained on youths' arrest charges and delinquency and dependency referral histories. Voluntary hair samples were provided by 94 percent of the youths to test for recent drug use.

Statistical Analyses

The main comparison groups of interest to our analysis involved n = 154 Extended Services youths, n = 70 youths not completing the FEI, and n = 79 youths completing the FEI. The decision not to continue receiving FEI services was made by the family. Field Consultants did not close any case due to a target youth's arrest or to development of a drug problem. On the contrary, these issues were considered important areas to address within the intervention and through appropriate referrals to community programs. In many cases, families moved out of the area or the parents/guardians were not willing or able to commit to participating in the family meetings. In several cases, the target youth was convicted on new charges and sentenced to an out-of-county state prison, precluding the continuance of family meetings. If the youth was in local custody (county jail or juvenile detention center), family meetings were held in these locations.

Subsequent Arrests for Delinquent/Criminal Offenses

For the analyses reported here, official records of contact with the juvenile justice system, adult arrests recorded in the information systems of the Florida Department of Law Enforcement, the Hillsborough County Jail System, and State Attorney of Hillsborough County, or involvement in the Florida Department of Corrections were obtained for each youth following his/her random assignment into the FEI or ESI groups. Two parallel analyses were completed on the official record data: (1) the number of offenses with which each youth was charged and (2) the number of arrests each youth experienced. Depending on the year youths entered the project, we collected and processed follow-up recidivism data covering one to four 12-month follow-up periods.

Number of Charges

In line with our previous work (Dembo, Williams, Schmeidler, & Christensen, 1993; Dembo, Ramirez-Garnica, Rollie, & Schmeidler, in press), we developed summary measures for the following offense categories: (1) *violent felonies*: murder/manslaughter, robbery, sex offenses, aggravated assault; (2) *property felonies*: arson, burglary, auto theft, larceny/theft, stolen property offenses, damaging property offenses; (3) *drug felonies*: drug offenses; (4) *violent misdemeanors*: nonaggravated assault; (5) *property misdemeanors*: larceny/theft, stolen property offenses, damaging property offenses; (6) *drug misdemeanors*: drug offenses; (7) *public disorder misdemeanors:* public disorder offenses, trespassing offenses; and (8) *the total number of charges across these offense categories*. For all offense categories except total charges, if an offense was of indeterminate seriousness, it was scored as 1/2 in each of the corresponding felony and misdemeanor summary measures.

Number of Arrests

Since a given arrest can involve multiple charges, we created a variable reflecting the total number of arrests as a juvenile or an adult during the follow-up period. A separate analysis was performed involving total number of arrests as a dependent variable.

Transformation of Data on Numbers of Charges and Numbers of Arrests

Before analyzing the number of charges or arrests, the data for each measure were separately transformed. We employed a square root transformation if there was any offense or arrest. If there was a charge or arrest, there was no correction for time at risk. Since reduced time at risk was almost invariably due to incarceration because of offenses, correction for time at risk would have penalized offenders twice. If there was no charge or arrest, the score was the negative of the square root of the years at risk. No charge or arrest in 12 months was assigned the score -1. The resulting scores emphasize the difference between offenders and nonoffenders, and de-emphasize time at risk for nonoffenders. All offenders were assigned positive scores and all nonoffenders negative scores (-1 for no offense in 1 year at risk). As the length of the follow-up period increases, the numbers of arrests and charges increase, but the negative score for nonoffenders also increases in magnitude. Using each youth's total charges and total arrests over a follow-up period of one to four years provided overall measures of recidivism. After transformation of the numbers of charges and arrests to adjust for time at risk among youths with no offenses, the means and standard deviations of the transformed scores are as follows: *number of charges*: $\bar{x} = 2.22$, standard deviation $= 1.32$; *number of arrests*: $\bar{x} = -0.06$; standard deviation $= 1.19$.

Table 1 shows the youths' rates of being charged for the seven specific offense categories, and their total charges across these categories, during various 12-month periods following the date of their random assignment into the FEI or ESI groups. The data shown in Table 1 suggest relatively few youths were charged with offenses in any of the seven offense-specific categories in any follow-up period, and the new charges generally declined from the first 12-month follow-up period to the fourth 12-month follow-up period. Hence, our analyses focused on the youths' total charges and total arrests.

Data Reduction

Preliminary data reductions were performed on the substantially interconnected sets of variables describing the youths' characteristics at entry. As a further data reduction procedure, principal components analysis was performed on 23 of the youths' psychosocial (e.g., lifetime reported use of marijuana, self-reported delinquency), official delinquency, and abuse-neglect referral history variables. Seven psychosocial, delinquency history, and abuse-neglect

☐ Table 1: Percent of Project Youths Who Were Charged One or More Times on Various Types of Offenses During the 48 Months of Random Assignment[†]

	Follow-Up Period			
Charged One or More Times for:	Within 12 Months of Random Assignment (n = 303)	Within the Second 12 Months Following Random Assignment (n = 193)	Within the Third 12 Months Following Random Assignment (n = 118)	Within the Fourth 12 Months Following Random Assignment (n = 23)
Violent Felony Offenses	14%	9%	4%	4%
Property Felony Offenses	15%	14%	13%	9%
Drug Felony Offenses	6%	7%	6%	9%
Violent Misdemeanor Offenses	17%	8%	2%	0%
Property Misdemeanor Offenses	24%	14%	9%	9%
Drug Misdemeanor Offenses	8%	6%	8%	9%
Public Disorder Misdemeanor Offenses	14%	7%	7%	9%
Total Charges	48%	37%	27%	17%

†Offenses comprising each charge category are discussed in the text.

history varimax components, accounting for 54 of the variance, were identified in these data (Dembo, Ramirez-Garnica, Rollie, Schmeidler, Livingston, & Hartsfield, in press).

Comparison of the Three Groups at Entry

A discriminant analysis was completed comparing ESI youths, youths not completing the FEI, and youths completing the FEI on 14 entry variables (the seven psychosocial, delinquency history, and abuse-neglect history varimax components, and seven sociodemographic and referral history variables [age, gender, race, ethnicity, living situation, diversion, or other case and total number of previous delinquency referrals]). The results were as follows: Wilks' lambda = 0.892, chi-square = 33.65, df = 26, p = n.s. (function 1); Wilks' lambda = 0.970, chi-square = 9.08, df = 12, p = n.s. (function 2). In addition, there was no significant difference between the three groups on any of the variables. Based on these results, it was not deemed necessary to control statistically for possible differences at entry among these groups before examining the impact of the intervention on the youths' number of charges and number of arrests.

For each of the comparisons among groups: FEI vs. ESI, FEI completers vs. FEI non-completers, and FEI completers against all others, two-way analyses of variance (ANOVAs) were performed. One independent variable was the group difference of interest, the other was the number of years of follow-up. This two-way ANOVA removes variation associated with length of follow-up from the comparison of groups.

RESULTS

Demographic, Educational, and Treatment History

Most youths were male (55%) and averaged 15 years of age. Fifty-nine percent of the youths were Anglo; 39 percent were African-American. Twenty-seven percent of the youths were Latino. Seventeen percent of the youths indicated they lived with both their biological parents; 64 percent indicated they resided with either their mother only (50%) or their mother and another adult (14%). Information on the occupational status of the household chief wage earner or other sources of household income (derived from Fishburne, Abelson, & Cisin, 1980), a measure of socioeconomic status, highlighted the low to moderate SES of the youths' families. Among the youths with codable data (n = 224), 14 percent of the chief wage earners held an executive, administrative/managerial, or professional specialty type position; 50 percent held unskilled, semiskilled, or low/moderate skilled service occupations; 13 percent of the youths' households were supported by public funds.

Although most of the youths (87%) were still attending school, many were experiencing educational problems. For example, 42 percent of the youths indicated they had been placed in a special educational program (e.g., Emotionally Handicapped, Specific Learning Disability) and 50 percent noted they had repeated a grade in school. Most youths lagged one (42%) or two (21%) grade levels behind the grade level that would be expected based on their chronological age. Only 20 percent of the youths reported that they ever received mental health care; fewer (6%) reported ever receiving substance abuse treatment.

Family Problem Characteristics

Many youths come from families with a number of difficulties in psychosocial functioning. Thirty-five percent of the youths reported that at least one member of their family or household family, besides themselves, had an alcohol abuse problem; 25 percent noted a family or household family member had another drug abuse problem (most frequently marijuana/hashish); and 24 percent indicated a family or household member had experienced an emotional or mental health problem.

In addition, members of the youths' families or household families often had different types of experience with the juvenile or adult justice systems. Sixty-six percent of the youths claimed at least one member of their family or household family, besides themselves, had been arrested, and from 45 to 57 percent reported that a member of their family/household family had been held in jail/detention, adjudicated delinquent, or convicted of a crime or put on community control or probation. Further, 34 percent of the youths noted at least one family member or household family member had been sent to a training school or prison.

A principal components analysis was completed on the family member alcohol abuse, other drug abuse, emotional/mental health problem, and contact with the justice system variables to see how they clustered. Two principal components were identified in this initial analysis (eigenvalues above 1.0, 3.92, and 1.38), which were rotated using varimax criteria for factor clarity. The two factors that were identified in the data were: (1) family member involvement with the justice system and (2) family member alcohol, other drug abuse, or mental health problems. Summary regression factor scores (Kim & Mueller, 1978) were created for further analysis. For each factor, higher scores indicated more family problems.

Friends' Substance Use and Involvement with the Police or Courts

Fifty-seven percent of the youths noted that one or more of their close friends had used alcohol, 51 percent marijuana/hashish, 14 percent hallucinogens, and seven percent cocaine, during the year prior to their initial interview. Further, large proportions of the youths' close friends had some type of contact with the legal system. Sixty-seven percent of the youths claimed at least one of their close friends had been arrested, and from 44 percent to 52 percent indicated that one or more of their close friends had been held in jail or detention, adjudicated delinquent or convicted of a crime, or been put on community control or probation. In addition, 15 percent of the youths reported that at least one of their close friends had been sent to a training school or prison.

A principal components analysis was completed on the friends' substance use and justice system contact variables as a data reduction technique and to see how they clustered. (Low frequency behaviors, such as reported friends' use of heroin, were excluded from this factor analysis.) Two principal components had eigenvalues above 1.0, 4.16, and 1.48, which were rotated using varimax criteria for factor clarity. The two factors that were identified in the data were: (1) friends' involvement with the justice system and (2) friends' drug use (alcohol, marijuana/hashish, hallucinogens, cocaine). Regression factor scores (Kim & Mueller, 1978) were created as a summary measure for further analysis. The higher the score, the more the reported friends' involvement with the justice system and/or drug use.

Physical Abuse

Drawing upon the work of Straus and his associates (Straus, 1979, 1983; Straus, Gelles, & Steinmetz, 1980), we used six items designed to determine the youths' physical abuse experiences. The youths were asked whether they had ever: (1) been beaten or *really* hurt by being hit (but not with anything) (24%); (2) been beaten or hit with a whip, strap, or belt (37%); (3) been beaten or hit with something "hard" (like a club or stick) (14%); (4) been shot with a gun, injured with a knife, or had some other "weapon" used against them (5%); (5) been hurt badly enough to require (need) a doctor or bandages or other medical treatment (10%); and (6) spent time in a hospital because they were physically injured (4%). Normative data on this behavior are difficult to obtain. However, available information from the 1995 national survey on family violence (Straus, Hamby, Finkelhor, Moore, & Runyan, 1998) found parent-to-child violence prevalence rates for being hit with something (5%), beat up (0.6%), or threatened with a knife or gun (0.1%) that were lower than those reported by the youths we interviewed.

As a data reduction procedure (Kim & Mueller, 1978), a principal components analysis was undertaken on the six physical abuse items. Two principal components with eigenvalues greater than 1.0, 2.43, and 1.05 were identified in these data. These two clusters were varimax rotated for factor clarity. The two factors that were identified were: (1) serious physical harm (above listed items 3 to 6 loaded highly on this factor) and (2) being beaten or hit (items 1 and 2 loaded highly on this factor). On the basis of these results, regression factor scores were created (Kim & Mueller, 1978). For each factor, higher scores indicated more different modes of physical harm claimed.

Sexual Victimization

Drawing upon the work of Finkelhor (1979), the youths were asked a number of the questions regarding their sexual experience. Each youth was asked if he or she ever had a sexual experience such as showing sex organs, touching sex organs, or intercourse. Respondents answering "yes" to this question were asked how many of these experiences they had had. Consistent with Finkelhor's (1979) operational definition, all youths who were 13 years of age or younger at the time of a sexual experience with a person over the age of 18 were considered to have been sexually victimized. In addition, youths who had a sexual experience at any age and who reported they were forced or threatened, had reacted to the experience with fear or shock, or had this experience with their parent, stepparent, or grandparent were also considered to have been sexually victimized. In line with this operational definition, consenting relationships between, for example, youths aged 14 to 17 years and an adult would not be classified as sexual abuse. Twenty-six percent of the youths had been sexually victimized at least once in their lives (34% of the females and 19% of the males, chi square = 8.62, df = 1, p < .001).

This rate of sexual victimization is comparable to the rate Mouzakitis (1981) found among the Arkansas training school girls he studied. It is also similar to the rate reported by youths involved in the Tampa longitudinal study of juvenile detainees (Dembo, Williams, & Schmeidler, 1998).

Self-Reported Alcohol and Illicit Drug Use Prior to Initial Interview

A number of questions on substance use were adopted from the National Household Survey on Drug Abuse (NHSDA) (National Institute on Drug Abuse, 1985) to determine the youths' use of various categories of substances: tobacco, alcohol, marijuana/hashish in non-blunt form, marijuana in blunt form, inhalants, hallucinogens, cocaine, heroin and the nonmedical use of barbiturates and other sedatives, tranquilizers, stimulants, and analgesics. The youths' use of tobacco is not considered in this article.

Our analysis of the alcohol use data focused on the youths' responses to a question probing the number of times in the past 12 months they reported being very high or drunk on alcohol. The data indicate that 19 percent of the youths reported they had gotten very high or drunk on alcohol 12 or more days in the preceding 12 months.

Questions concerning the youths' illicit drug use or nonmedical use of psychotherapeutic drugs probed their age of first use, lifetime frequency of use, and recency of use. The present analyses focus on the youths' reported lifetime frequency of drug use. Over half (57%) of the youths reported using marijuana in non-blunt form and almost as many (51%) in blunt form. No other drug was used by more than 14 percent of the youths.

Eighteen percent of the youths claimed to have used marijuana/hashish in reefer form, and 13 percent marijuana in blunt form, 100 or more times in their lives. Since the reported lifetime frequency of marijuana/hashish use in non-blunt form (e.g., reefers) and in blunt form was strongly associated (r = .666, n = 303, p < .001), a composite index of the youths' marijuana/hashish use was created, summing standardized scores for these two variables. The drug use prevalence rates were, with one exception (the nonmedical use of analgesics), higher than those reported by the 12 to 17-year-old youths interviewed in the 1996 National Household Survey on Drug Abuse (Substance Abuse and Mental Health Services Administration, 1997). The NHSDA survey found the following prevalence rates for the nine categories of illicit drugs (given in parentheses): marijuana/hashish–57% (vs. 17% in the NHSDA sample), inhalants–9% (vs. 6%), hallucinogens–14% (vs. 6%), cocaine–12% (vs. 2%), heroin–2% (vs. 0.5%), nonmedical use of sedatives–3% (vs. 1%), tranquilizers–27% (vs. 2%), stimulants–7% (vs. 2%), and analgesics–4% (vs. 6%).

Self-Reported Delinquent Behavior

Drawing upon the work of Elliott, Ageton, Huizinga, Knowles, and Canter (1983), we probed the youths' delinquent behavior in the year prior to their initial interviews by asking how many times they engaged in 23 delinquent behaviors. In addition, as a check, youths noting they had engaged in a given act 10 or more times were asked to indicate how often they participated in this behavior (once a month, once every two or three weeks, once a week, two to three times a week, once a day, or two to three times a day). In addition, for each of the 23 delinquent behaviors in which the youth claimed to have engaged, he/she was asked the age during which the act first occurred.

Based on the youths' claimed frequency of participation in the various delinquent acts, we developed the following four summary indices of the youngsters' delinquent involvement used by Elliott and his associates (1983):

- General Theft: stole a motor vehicle, stole something worth more than $50, bought stolen goods, stole something worth less than $5, stole something worth between $5 and $50, broke into a building or vehicle, joyriding.
- Crimes Against Persons: aggravated assault, gang fights, hit a teacher, hit a parent, hit a student, sexual assault, strong-armed students, strong-armed teachers, strong-armed others.
- Index crimes: aggravated assault, sexual assault, gang fights, stole a motor vehicle, stole something worth more than $50, broke into a building or vehicle, strong-armed students, strong-armed teachers, strong-armed others.
- Total Delinquency: the sum of the reported frequency of participation in the 23 delinquent activities.

In addition, we constructed a drug sales index for analysis as follows:

• Drug Sales: sold marijuana or hashish, sold cocaine or crack, sold other hard drugs such as heroin or LSD.

The self-reported delinquency frequency rates for the 303 youths during the year prior to their interviews indicated high prevalence rates for index offenses (56%), crimes against persons (65%), general theft (82%), drug sales (26%), and total delinquency (94%). Further, from 2 to 16 percent of the youths reported engaging in the offenses represented by the various scales 100 times or more–some reported many hundreds of offenses.

Since the range of responses to the items comprising the five self-reported delinquency scales was large, ranging from no activity to hundreds (and in a few cases thousands), analysis of the frequency data as an interval scale was not appropriate as a measure of involvement in delinquency/crime. Raw numbers of offenses do form an interval scale, which might be useful if one were predicting crime rates for populations. However, the difference between no offense and one offense is not the same as the difference between 99 and 100 offenses in terms of involvement. A transformation was employed so that equal intervals on the transformed scale would represent equal differences in involvement. We interpreted the differences between 1 and 10, 10 and 100, and 100 and 1000 offenses as being comparable. Accordingly, we log transformed the number of offenses for each scale to the base 10.

For any base, logarithms exist for all positive numbers. The choice of base does not matter, if the logarithms are analyzed by a statistical procedure invariant under linear transformation, such as analysis of variance, multiple regression, discriminant analysis, or factor analysis. However, regardless of the base, the logarithm of zero does not exist. Some other method must be employed to determine the score assigned to no offenses. For any base, zero is the logarithm of the value one, and one is the logarithm of the base. If the difference from "base" offenses (10 in this study) to one offense is assigned the difference in logarithm scores of one and zero, this provides a unit of measurement for assigning a score even lower than zero–a negative number–to no offenses. In this study a score of minus one was assigned. This evaluates the difference between no offense and one offense as equal in importance as the difference between 1 offense and 10, or 10 offenses and 100.

Emotional/Psychological Functioning

The SCL-90-R (Derogatis, 1983) was used to assess the youths' emotional/psychological functioning. The youths' replies to the items yielded T scores on nine symptom dimensions: (1) somatization–distress arising from perceptions of bodily dysfunction; (2) obsessive-compulsive–symptoms that are closely identified with the standard clinical syndrome of the same name; (3) interpersonal sensitivity–feelings of personal inadequacy and inferiority, particularly in comparisons with others; (4) depression–a broad range of manifestations of clinical depression; (5) anxiety–a set of symptoms and signs that are associated clinically with high levels of manifest anxiety; (6) hostility–thoughts, feelings, or actions that are characteristic of the negative affect state of anger; (7) phobic anxiety–persistent fear of a specific person, place, object, or situation, characterized as irrational and disproportionate to the stimulus, leading to avoidance or escape behavior; (8) paranoid ideation–a disoriented mode of thinking; and (9) psychotocism–includes a range of items tapping functioning from mild interpersonal alienation to dramatic evidence of psychosis.

T-score means of the nine SCL-90-R scales were all 47.2 or lower. Comparison to the mean of 50 and standard deviation of 10 in the standardizing population indicated the T-scores for the nine scales were significantly lower than the standardizing population (adolescent non-patients) at the .001 significance level.

A principal components analysis was performed on the SCL-90-R T-scores for the nine scales to see how they clustered. One main principal component was identified in these data. Each of the scales loaded significantly on this main component, which accounted for 74 percent of the variance. Regression factor scores (Kim & Mueller, 1978) were created summarizing these data. The higher the score, the more emotional/psychological problems.

Arrest Charges upon Entering JAC

Almost all youths entered JAC as a result of being taken into custody on one or more felony or misdemeanor charges. Most of the charges on the youths were felony property charges (51%) (especially burglary, grand larceny, and auto theft). Misdemeanor property charges (e.g., retail theft) ranked second (40%). Seventeen percent of the youths were brought to JAC on violent felony charges (e.g., robbery). Relatively few youths were arrested on drug felony (7%) or misdemeanor (5%) charges, or on public disorder misdemeanor (8%) or violent misdemeanor (1%) charges.

Referral History

Information obtained from the Florida Department of Juvenile Justice (DJJ) indicated 25 percent of the youths were referred to juvenile court at least once for property felony offenses (e.g., burglary), 36 percent for misdemeanor property offenses (e.g., retail theft), 22 percent for misdemeanor violent offenses, 18 percent for felony violence (e.g., robbery), and 17 percent for misdemeanor public disorder offenses (e.g., trespassing). The youths were victims as well as offenders. Seventeen percent had been referred to the Florida Department of Health and Rehabilitative Services for being physically abused and 17 percent for being neglected.

A principal components analysis was completed on the delinquency referral variables to see how they clustered. The initial solution, involving two factors with eigenvalues greater than 1.0, 2.34, and 1.43, was rotated to varimax criteria for factor clarity. The two factors that were identified in these data were: (1) violence, property, and public disorder offenses and (2) drug offenses. Based on these results, regression factor scores were calculated (Kim & Mueller, 1978). Higher scores on each factor indicated more frequent referrals.

Hair Testing for Substance Use

An important part of the youths' interviews was obtaining hair specimens for analysis for recent drug use. About one and a half inch of hair is collected across a finger and cut as close to the scalp as possible. The hair specimens were prepared for shipment following the established protocol of Psychemedics Corporation in Culver City, California, and were processed by them.

Psychemedics performed RIAH® testing of the hair samples for past 90 days use of the following substances: cocaine, opiates, PCP, methphetamines, and marijuana. The cutoff for a positive for cocaine and methamphetamines was 5 ng/10 mg hair; for PCP it was 3 ng/10 mg of hair; for opiates it was 2 ng/10 mg of hair; and for marijuana it was 10 pg carboxy-THC equivalents/10 mg of hair. (In a few cases where hair was not available, fingernail samples were collected and analyzed.) In the case of cocaine and opiates, the antibody used in the radioimmunoassay does not produce any false positive results. With the marijuana radioimmunoassay, between 5 to 10 percent of positive results may be false positives as a result of hair matrix effects near the cutoff level of the assay. False negatives are determined by the values of the cutoff level. For cocaine, individuals using less than 1 to 3 lines of cocaine per month are reported as negative. For opiates, individuals using less than two bags of heroin per week are scored as negative. For marijuana, because of its 100,000 lower concentration in hair than cocaine, it appears that only the heavy and moderate, but not the light user, is identified by the hair assay. The exact clinical definitions of these categories of use have not been defined to date (Baumgartner & Hill, 1996).

The results of the hair/nail testing were striking. Forty-six percent of the 286 youths tested (no test results were available for 17 youths) were positive on one or more of the five drugs: 32 percent were positive on one drug (marijuana [22%] or cocaine [9%]), 13 percent were positive on two drugs (marijuana and cocaine [12%], marijuana and opiates [1%]), and 1 percent were positive on marijuana, cocaine, and opiates. Overall, 36 percent of the youths were positive on marijuana, and 22 percent were positive on cocaine.

Recidivism Comparison of the Three Groups

Using transformed variables that adjusted for time at risk for non-offenders, FEI youths had fewer charges (mean = $-.08$) and arrests (mean = $-.15$) than ESI youths (mean charges = .12, mean arrests = .02). A further indication of the impact of the intervention was that youths who completed the FEI had fewer charges (mean = $-.17$) and arrests (mean = $-.25$) than those who did not complete the FEI (mean charges = .03, mean arrests = $-.04$). In an additional comparison, youths who did not complete the FEI together with ESI youths had more charges (mean = .09) and arrests (mean = 0) than youths who completed the FEI (mean charges = $-.17$, mean arrests = $-.25$). Table 2 presents results of the ANOVAs for these comparisons.

All differences between groups were in the predicted direction, and the FEI youths who completed the intervention had marginally significantly fewer transformed charges ($F = 1.93$; df = 1,141; p = .083–1-sided) and very close to significantly fewer transformed arrests ($F = 2.71$; df = 1,141; p = .051–1-sided) than youths not completing the FEI. Different numbers of charges or arrests for youths with different lengths of follow-up reflect the tendency for more offenses to occur in longer periods of time, which was mitigated but not eliminated by the transformations. It is noteworthy that there were no significant interactions of group differences with length of follow-up. This indicates that overall differences among groups did not vary substantially for different lengths of follow-up.

Time and Treatment Group by Time Effects on the Recidivism Measures

Additional analyses were performed to determine the effect of length of follow-up time on the number of charges and number of arrests and to separately assess the interaction between each of the three comparison groups (defined as shown in Table 2) by the number of charges and number of arrests over time in regard to total number of charges and total number of arrests, respectively. As suggested in Table 1, statistically significant reductions in number of charges and number of arrests occurred over time. However, no statistically significant comparison group by recidivism measure interaction effects were found.

☐ **Table 2: Comparison of Recidivism Measures Across Extended Services Youths, Youths Not Completing the FEI, and Youths Completing the FEI** [†]

Source of Variation	df	Transformed Charges					Transformed Arrests			
		SS	MS	F	p*		SS	MS	F	p*
FEI vs. ESI	1	.11	.11	.04	.423		.00	.00	.00	.500
Years of follow-up	3	27.10	9.03	3.09	.027		13.74	4.58	1.99	.116
Interaction	3	8.20	2.73	.94	.424		7.66	2.55	1.11	.346
Error	295	862.06	2.92				679.39	2.30		
FEI completed vs. FEI not completed	1	5.47	5.47	1.93	.083		6.27	6.27	2.71	.051
Years of follow-up	3	17.49	5.83	2.06	.108		12.25	4.08	1.77	.156
Interaction	3	12.17	4.06	1.43	.235		9.13	3.04	1.32	.271
Error	141	399.10	2.83				325.84	2.31		
FEI completed vs. all other youths	1	2.50	2.50	.86	.177		2.15	2.15	.93	.168
Years of follow-up	3	28.20	9.40	3.23	.023		16.03	5.34	2.32	.075
Interaction	3	5.84	1.95	.67	.572		3.95	1.32	.57	.633
Error	295	859.52	2.91				678.47	2.30		

*Tests of differences between groups were one-sided. Other tests were not directional.
†The variables used in these analyses were coded as follows: the total number of arrest charges and total number of arrests: higher scores indicate more recidivism reflected in the measure, controlling for the youths' time at risk.

The Influence of Change of Project Clinical Leadership on the Recidivism Data

The clinical leadership of the project changed in March 1996, at which time the clinical director was replaced by a clinical coordinator and two line supervisors. Hence, a dummy coded variable was created, reflecting whether families entered the project prior to (0) or subsequent to (1) March 1996. This variable was incorporated in two ANOVAs relating to total number of charges and number of arrests. These analyses indicated this time-of-entry-into-the-project variable did not have an appreciable effect on the results we reported earlier.

DISCUSSION AND CONCLUSIONS

Overall, the results of our analysis indicate that youths completing the FEI had marginally significant lower total arrest charges and total number of arrests over the follow-up period than youths not competing the FEI. These results support the efficacy of the intervention, although at a more modest level than in our 12-month recidivism study (Dembo, Ramirez-Garnica, Rollie, Schmeidler, Livingston, & Hartsfield, in press). An alternative explanation is that youths did better because they were amenable to intervention, rather than as the effect of the intervention. However, if this were the case, one would expect that there would be other differences in Time 1 characteristics, which was not the case.

These important effects are presented in more visible fashion in Figures 1 and 2, which display the mean values for transformed new charges (Figure 1) and transformed new arrests (Figure 2) for ESI youths, youths not completing the FEI, and youths completing the FEI. As can be seen, ESI youths, on aver-

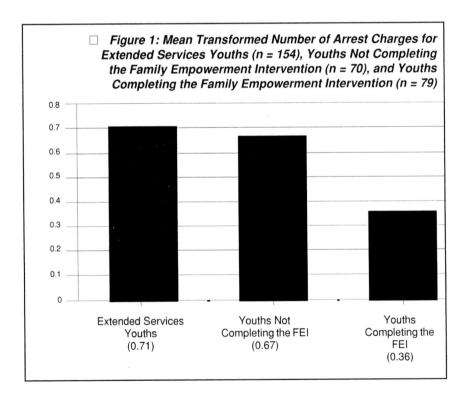

Figure 1: Mean Transformed Number of Arrest Charges for Extended Services Youths (n = 154), Youths Not Completing the Family Empowerment Intervention (n = 70), and Youths Completing the Family Empowerment Intervention (n = 79)

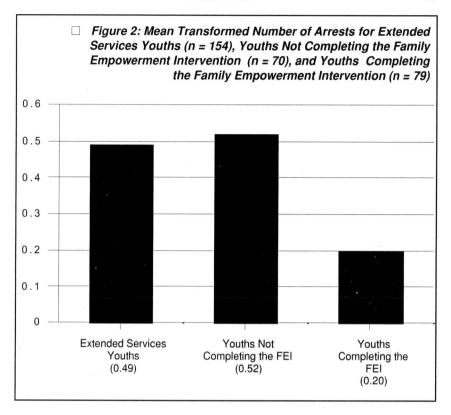

Figure 2: Mean Transformed Number of Arrests for Extended Services Youths (n = 154), Youths Not Completing the Family Empowerment Intervention (n = 70), and Youths Completing the Family Empowerment Intervention (n = 79)

age, had 0.71 new charges, compared to 0.67 new charges for youths not completing the FEI and 0.36 new charges for youths completing the FEI. Further, ESI youths, on average, had 0.49 new arrests, compared to 0.52 new arrests for youths not completing the FEI and 0.20 new arrests for youths completing the FEI. Compared to ESI youths and youths not completing the FEI combined, youths completing the FEI had a 48 percent *lower* rate of new charges and a 60 percent *lower* rate of new arrests.

The long-term effects of the FEI are less robust than the 12-month impact of the intervention on youth recidivism (see: Dembo, Ramirez-Garnica, Rollie, Schmeidler, Livingston, & Hartsfield in press). Since the intervention was designed to be short-term, and no additional services were systematically applied following completion of the FEI, the long-term outcome effects we found were gratifying. We believe the strength of the long-term effect of the intervention could have been enhanced by periodic booster sessions designed to support target youth and family maintenance of their intervention gains. Other analyses have documented the long-term beneficial effects of the FEI in regard to the youths' psychosocial outcomes covering a 36-month post-initial interview period. In particular, reductions in drug use and self-reported delinquency were found (Dembo, Schmeidler et al., in preparation).

The long-term recidivism findings are particularly important in light of the experience that the salutary effects of intervention programs for high-risk youths are, unfortunately, often short-lived. The University of Colorado Center for the Study and Prevention of Violence (1999) notes that treatment or intervention gains of most programs are lost after participation in the intervention or soon thereafter. The intervention effects we found are consistent with the main hypothesis of this project. Further, substantial justice system direct cost savings can be anticipated by use of this intervention (see: Dembo, Ramirez-Garnica, Rollie, Schmeidler, Livingston, & Hartsfield, in press). We hope the continued documented value of this attractive, cost-efficient intervention will encourage its implementation in other jurisdictions.

REFERENCES

Alexander, J.F., & Parsons, B.V. (1982). *Functional Family Therapy: Principles and Procedures*. Carmel, CA: Brooks/Cole.

Arcia, E., Keyes, L., Gallagher, J.J., & Herrick, H. (1993). National portrait of sociodemographic factors associated with underutilization of services: Relevance to early intervention. *Journal of Early Intervention, 17*, 283-297.

Baumgartner, W., & Hill, V. (1996). Hair analysis for organic analyses: Methodology, reliability issues, and field studies. In P. Kintz (ed.)., *Drug Testing in Hair*. New York: CRC Press.

Bronfenbrenner, U. (1979). *The Ecology of Human Development: Experiments by Nature and Design*. Cambridge, MA: Harvard University Press.

Cervenka, K.A., Dembo, R., & Brown, C.H. (1996). A Family Empowerment Intervention for families of juvenile offenders. *Aggression and Violent Behavior, 1*, 205-216.

Christenson, A., & Jacobson, N.S. (1994). Who (or what) can do psychotherapy: The status and challenge of non-professional therapies. *Psychological Science, 5*, 8-14.

Dembo, R., & Brown, R. (1994). The Hillsborough County Juvenile Assessment Center. *Journal of Child and Adolescent Substance Abuse, 3*, 25-43.

Dembo, R., Pacheco, K., Schmeidler, J., Fisher, L., & Cooper, S. (1997). Drug use and delinquent behavior among high risk youths. *Journal of Child and Adolescent Substance Abuse, 6*, 1-25.

Dembo, R., Ramirez-Garnica, G., Rollie, M., & Schmeidler, J. (In press). Impact of a Family Empowerment Intervention on youth recidivism. *Journal of Offender Rehabilitation*.

Dembo, R., Ramirez-Garnica, G., Rollie, M., Schmeidler, J., Livingston, S., & Hartsfield, A. (In press). Youth recidivism 12 months after a Family Empowerment Intervention: Final report. *Journal of Offender Rehabilitation.*

Dembo, R., Schmeidler, J., Seeberger, W., Shemwell, M., Livingston, S., Rollie, M., Pacheco, K., & Wothke, W. (In preparation). Long-term impact of a Family Empowerment Intervention on juvenile offender psychosocial functioning. Tampa: University of South Florida, Department of Criminology.

Dembo, R., Shemwell, M., Guida, J., Schmeidler, J., Pacheco, K., & Seeberger, W. (1998). A longitudinal study of the impact of a Family Empowerment Intervention on juvenile offender psychosocial functioning: A first assessment. *Journal of Child and Adolescent Substance Abuse, 8,* 15-54.

Dembo, R., Turner, G., Schmeidler, J., Chin Sue, C., Borden, P., & Manning, D. (1996). Development and evaluation of a classification of high risk youths entering a juvenile assessment center. *International Journal of the Addictions, 31,* 303-322.

Dembo, R., Williams, L., Berry, E., Getreu, A., Washburn, M., Wish, E.D., & Schmeidler, J. (1990). Examination of the relationships among drug use, emotional/psychological problems and crime among youths entering a juvenile detention center. *International Journal of the Addictions, 25,* 1301-1340.

Dembo, R., Williams, L., & Schmeidler, J. (1998). Key findings of the Tampa longitudinal study of juvenile detainees: Contributions to a theory of drug use and delinquency among high risk youths. In A.R. Roberts (ed.), *Juvenile Justice: Policies, Programs and Services,* 2nd edition. Chicago: Nelson-Hall.

Dembo, R., Williams, L., Schmeidler, J., & Christensen, C. (1993). Recidivism in a cohort of juvenile detainees. *International Journal of the Addictions, 28,* 631-657.

Dembo, R., Williams, L., Schmeidler, J., & Howitt, D. (1991). *Tough Cases: School Outreach for At-Risk Youth.* Washington, DC: US Department of Education, Office of the Assistant Secretary for Educational Research and Improvement.

Dembo, R., Williams, L., Wothke, W., Schmeidler, J., & Brown, C.H. (1992). The role of family factors, physical abuse and sexual victimization experiences in high risk youths' alcohol and other drug use and delinquency: A longitudinal model. *Violence and Victims, 7,* 245-266.

Dembo, R., Wothke, W., Shemwell, M., Pacheco, K., Seeberger, W., Rollie, M., & Schmeidler, J. (In press). The relationships of high risk youth family problems and their problem behavior: A structural model. *Journal of Child and Adolescent Substance Abuse.*

Derogatis, L.D. (1983). *SCL-90-R Administration, Scoring and Procedures Manual.* Towson, MD: Clinical Psychometric Research.

Elliott, D.S., Ageton, S.S., Huizinga, D., Knowles, B.A., & Canter, R.J. (1983). *The Prevalence and Incidence of Delinquent Behavior: 1976-1980.* Boulder, CO: Behavioral Research Institute.

Finkelhor, D. (1979). *Sexually Victimized Children.* New York: Free Press.

Fishburn, P.M., Abelson, H.I., & Cisin, I. (1980). *National Survey on Drug Abuse: Main Findings–1979.* Rockville, MD: National Institute on Drug Abuse.

Henggeler, S.W., & Borduin, C.M. (1990). *Family Therapy and Beyond: A Multisystemic Approach to Treating the Behavior Problems of Children and Adolescents*. Pacific Grove, CA: Brooks/Cole.

Henggeler, S.W., Melton, G.B., Smith, L.A., Schoenwald, S.W., & Hanley, J.H. (1993). Family preservation using multi-systemic treatment: Long term follow-up to a clinical trial with serious juvenile offenders. *Journal of Child and Family Studies, 2*, 283-293.

Henggeler, S.W., Schoenwald, S.K., Pickrel, S.G., Brondino, M.J., Borduin, C.M., & Hall, J.A. (1994). *Treatment Manual for Family Preservation Using Multisystemic Therapy*. Charleston, SC: Medical University of South Carolina.

Kim, J., & Mueller, C.E. (1978). *Factor Analysis: Statistical Methods and Practical Issues*. Beverly Hills, CA: Sage.

Klitzner, M., Fisher, D., Stewart, K., & Gilbert, S. (1991). *Report to the Robert Wood Johnson Foundation on Strategies for Early Intervention with Children and Youth to Avoid Abuse of Addictive Substances*. Bethesda, MD: Pacific Institute for Research and Evaluation.

Kumpfer, K., & Alvarado, R. (1998). *Effective Family Strengthening Interventions*. Washington, DC: U.S. Department of Justice. NCJ 171121.

Le Blanc, M. (1990, September). *Family Dynamics, Adolescent Delinquency and Adult Criminality*. Paper presented at the Society for Life History Research Conference. Keystone, CO.

Mouzakitis, C.W. (1981). Inquiry into the problem of child abuse and juvenile delinquency. In R.J. Hunner & Y.E. Walker (eds.), *Exploring the Relationship Between Child Abuse and Delinquency*. Montclair, NJ: Allenheld, Osmun and Co.

National Institute on Drug Abuse (1985). *1985 National Household Survey on Drug Abuse Questionnaire*. Rockville, MD: National Institute on Drug Abuse.

Nurco, D.N., Balter, M.B., & Kinlock, T. (1994). Vulnerability to narcotic addiction. *Journal of Drug Issues, 24*, 293-314.

Office of National Drug Control Policy (1997). *What America's Users Spend on Illegal Drugs, 1988-1995*. Washington, DC: ONDCP.

Rahdert, E., & Czechowicz, D. (Eds.) (1995). *Adolescent Drug Abuse: Clinical Assessment and Therapeutic Interventions*. Rockville, MD: National Institute on Drug Abuse.

Sherman, L., Gottfredson, D., MacKenzie, D., Eck, J., Reuten, P., & Bushway, S. (1997). *Preventing Crime: What Works, What Doesn't, What's Promising?* College Park, MD: University of Maryland, Dept. of Criminology and Criminal Justice.

Sirles, E.A. (1990). Dropout from intake, diagnostics, and treatment. *Community Mental Health Journal, 26*, 345-360.

Straus, M.A. (1979). Measuring intrafamily conflict and violence: The conflict tactics (CT) scales. *Journal of Marriage and the Family, 41*, 75-88.

Straus, M.A. (1983). Ordinary violence, child abuse, and wife-beating, What do they have in common? In D. Finkelhor, R.J. Gelles, G.T. Hotaling, & M.A. Straus (eds.), *The Dark Side of Families: Current Family Violence Research*. Beverly Hills, CA: Sage.

Straus, M.A., Gelles, R.J., & Steinmetz, S.K. (1980). *Behind Closed Doors: Violence in the American Family*. New York: Doubleday/Anchor.

Straus, M., Hamby, S.L., Finkelhor, D., Moore, D., & Runyan, D. (1998). Identification of child maltreatment with parent-child Conflict Tactics Scales: Development and psychometric data for a national sample of American parents. *Child Abuse and Neglect, 22*, 249-270.

Substance Abuse and Mental Health Services Administration (SAMHSA) (1997). *Preliminary Data from the 1996 National Household Survey on Drug Abuse.* Rockville, MD: SAMHSA.

Szapocznik, J., & Kurtines, W.M. (1989). *Breakthroughs in Family Therapy with Drug-Abusing and Problem Youth.* New York: Springer Publishing Co.

Teplin, L.A., & Swartz, J. (1989). Screening for severe mental disorder in jails: The development of the referral decision scale. *Law and Human Behavior, 13,* 1-18.

Tolan, P., Ryan, K., & Jaffe, C. (1988). Adolescents' mental health service use and provider, process, and recipient characteristics. *Journal of Clinical Child Psychology, 17,* 229-236.

University of Colorado Center for the Study and Prevention of Violence Model Program Selection Criteria. (1999). Available FTP: 128.138.129.25. File: <www.colorado.edu/cspu/blueprints/about/criteria.htm>.

Weisz, J.R., Weiss, B., Han, S.S., Granger, D.A., & Norton (1995). Effects of psychotherapy with children and adolescents revisited: A meta-analysis of treatment outcome studies. *Psychological Bulletin, 117,* 450-468.

AUTHORS' NOTES

Richard Dembo, PhD, is a professor of Criminology at the University of South Florida in Tampa. He has a long-term interest in developing, implementing, and evaluating intervention programs for high-risk youths.

Gabriela Ramirez-Garnica, MPH, is a doctoral candidate in Epidemiology at the Department of Epidemiology and Biostatistics, College of Public Health at the University of South Florida in Tampa. Her areas of interest are drug abuse, behavioral, and HIV/AIDS epidemiology.

James Schmeidler, PhD, is an assistant clinical professor in the Department of Psychiatry and Biomathematical Sciences at the Mt. Sinai School of Medicine. He has considerable experience applying statistical procedures to behavioral science data.

Matthew Rollie, BS, is a graduate assistant in the Department of Criminology at the University of South Florida. He is currently a student at the University of South Florida College of Public Health in the Department of Environmental Health, and is working on his masters degree in Tropical Public Health/Infectious Diseases.

Stephen Livingston, BA, is a research assistant in the Department of Criminology at the University of South Florida. He has been associated with the Youth Support Project since 1998.

Amy Hartsfield, BA, is a graduate assistant in the Department of Criminology at the University of South Florida. She is interested in biological factors in delinquency.

The preparation of this manuscript was supported by Grant #1-RO1-DA08707, funded by the National Institute on Drug Abuse. The authors are grateful for their support. However, the research results reported and the views expressed in the article do not necessarily imply any policy or research endorsement by our funding agency.

The authors would like to thank clinical, intervention, and other research staff for their contributions to this project. Great thanks are due to project Field Consultants for their work. The authors deeply appreciate the support of Mr. Darrell Manning, supervisor of the Juvenile Assessment Center; he was a great resource to the work. The authors are grateful for Dr. Werner Wothke's assistance on the strategy of analysis section. The authors also deeply appreciate Ms. Marianne Bell's word processing of this manuscript.

Address correspondence to Richard Dembo, PhD, Criminology Department, University of South Florida, 4202 E. Fowler Avenue, Tampa, FL 33620.

Family Empowerment as an Intervention Strategy in Juvenile Delinquency. Pp. 59-109.

Long-Term Impact
of a Family Empowerment Intervention
on Juvenile Offender Psychosocial Functioning

RICHARD DEMBO

Department of Criminology, University of South Florida, Tampa

JAMES SCHMEIDLER

Departments of Psychiatry and Biomathematical Sciences, Mt. Sinai School of Medicine, New York

WILLIAM SEEBERGER

Department of Criminology, University of South Florida, Tampa

MARINA SHEMWELL

Department of Criminology, University of South Florida, Tampa

MATTHEW ROLLIE

Department of Environmental and Occupational Health, University of South Florida, Tampa

KIMBERLY PACHECO

Department of Criminology, University of South Florida, Tampa

STEPHEN LIVINGSTON

Department of Criminology, University of South Florida, Tampa

WERNER WOTHKE

Small Waters Corporation, Chicago

ABSTRACT We report the results of a study of the long-term impact of a Family Empowerment Intervention (FEI) on the psychosocial functioning among youths processed at the Hillsborough County Juvenile Assessment Center who entered the project between September 1, 1994 and January 31, 1998. The FEI seeks to improve family functioning by empowering parents. Families involved in the project were randomly assigned to either receive an Extended Services Intervention (ESI) or the FEI. Families in the ESI group received monthly phone contacts and, if indicated, referral information; FEI families received three one-hour, home-based meetings per week from a clinician-trained paraprofessional. The results provide support for the sustained effect of FEI services. Analysis indicated that youths who completed the FEI had statistically significant lower rates of reported getting very high or drunk on alcohol, and claimed frequency of participation in crimes against persons, drug sales, and total delinquency, at last observation, than youths not completing the FEI. The results add to the findings of our earlier 12-month psychosocial functioning outcome analyses, which provided strong evidence of the salutary effects of the FEI. *[Article copies available for a fee from The Haworth Document Delivery Service: 1-800-342-9678. E-mail address: <getinfo@haworthpressinc.com> Website: <http:// www.HaworthPress.com> © 2001 by The Haworth Press, Inc. All rights reserved.]*

KEYWORDS Juvenile offender psychosocial functioning, juvenile offender family intervention and long-term psychosocial outcomes, impact of family intervention on juvenile offender psychosocial functioning

INTRODUCTION

Developing effective intervention programs for youths involved in the juvenile justice system remains a top national priority (Sherman and Associates, 1997). Programs which respond to the needs of troubled youths in a holistic fashion are more likely to be successful (McBride, Vanderwall, Terry, & Van Buren, 1999). Innovative service delivery strategies are especially needed for minority and inner city youths and families who have been underserved in regard to their mental health and substance misuse service needs (Arcia, Keyes, Gallagher, & Herrick, 1993; Sirles, 1990; Tolan, Ryan, & Jaffe, 1988). In the absence of effective intervention services, all too many youths entering the juvenile justice system will move to the adult justice system and consume a large and growing amount of local, state, and national criminal justice and mental health resources as they grow older (Office of National Drug Control Policy, 1997). Early intervention holds promise of cost-effectively reducing the probability that troubled youths will continue criminal and high health-risk behavior into adulthood (Klitzner, Fisher, Stewart, & Gilbert, 1991).

Such programs need to reflect the experience that many youths entering the juvenile justice system have problems in the areas of physical abuse, sexual victimization, alcohol and other drug use, family relationships, school, and emotional/psychological functioning. Often, these youths' difficulties can be traced to family alcohol/other drug use, mental health, or crime problems which began at an early age (Dembo, Williams, & Schmeidler, 1998; Dembo, Wothke, Shemwell, Pacheco, Seeberger, Rollie, & Schmeidler, in press; Teplin & Swartz, 1989; Dembo, Williams, Berry, Getreu, Washburn, Wish, & Schmeidler, 1990; Dembo, Williams, Schmeidler, & Howitt, 1990; Dembo, Pacheco, Schmeidler, Fisher, & Cooper, 1997; Dembo, Williams, Wothke, Schmeidler, & Brown, 1992). These factors place youths at high risk for future drug use and delinquency/crime. Reaching youths in early adolescence, ideally at first contact with the justice system, provides an excellent opportunity to involve them in needed services before their problems become more serious.

Unfortunately, most communities lack sufficient screening, in-depth assessment, and treatment resources to respond effectively to the needs of troubled youths. As a result, too many youths fall through the cracks of the service delivery system. None of the expected benefits of treatment can occur unless youths become involved in, and participate in, care for a sufficient period of time for these experiences to have an impact. Service delivery challenges are particularly great among economically stressed families who lack the resources to pay for care, have not been effectively served by traditional service delivery systems, or are dependent on overburdened and under-resourced public services. It is unlikely that treatment resources will expand sufficiently in the next decade to meet the growing needs of these families. Innovative approaches are urgently needed to serve them.

Efforts are being made to develop interventions in which staff working with delinquent youths and their families are trained to provide services, and, if indicated, link them with additional community services. Such an approach holds promise of improving services made available to various high-risk youths and their families. A number of intervention efforts, focusing on family preservation and informed by an ecological systems view (Bronfenbrenner, 1979), are being implemented in various parts of the U.S. (e.g., Rahdert & Czechowicz, 1995; Kumpfer & Alvarado, 1998; Szapocznik & Kurtines, 1989). For example, multisystemic therapy (MST) has been found successful in addressing the needs of juvenile offenders and their families (Henggeler & Borduin, 1990; Henggeler, Melton, Smith, Schoenwald, & Hanley, 1993; Henggeler, Schoenwald, Pickrel, Brondino, Borduin, & Hall, 1994). Clinical trials of MST have involved service delivery at community mental health centers. Trained therapists have provided services to four to six "at-risk youths" and their families for as long as four to five months. The family preservation focus of MST seeks to "empower parents to restructure their environments in ways that promote development" (Henggeler, Schoenwald, Pickrel, Brondino, Borduin, & Hall, 1994, p. 21) by developing their parental competencies. From a structural family therapy perspective, an essential first step is to focus on the parents in order to restructure the family and establish parental control. A second goal is to teach the parents how to use agencies and services, including schools, more effectively (Henggeler et al., 1994).

Functional family therapy (Alexander & Parsons, 1982) has been found effective in treating youths 11 to 18 years of age who are involved in alcohol or other drug abuse or delinquent behavior, and in reducing justice and other service system costs in serving these youths. A wide range of trained interventionists, working in one or two person teams, provide from 8 to 26 hours of in-home services, involving five phases (engagement, motivation, assessment, behavior change, and generalization), to referred youths and their families.

Another innovative intervention is the Youth Support Project (YSP) in Tampa, Florida, a service delivery study funded by the National Institute on Drug Abuse, Division of Clinical Research. The study is in its final year. The goal of the project's Family Empowerment Intervention (FEI) is to improve family functioning through empowering parents. As discussed in more detail in the next section, YSP services are provided by trained paraprofessional staff working under the guidance of licensed clinicians. To our knowledge, the YSP is the largest clinical trial of its type ever undertaken involving this target group.

A recently completed final assessment of the 12-month psychosocial impact of this intervention on a cohort of 272 youths entering the project between September 1, 1994, and January 31, 1998, provided strong evidence of the beneficial effects of FEI services on the youths' drug use and delinquent behavior, particularly among youths who completed the intervention (Dembo, Seeberger, Shemwell, Schmeidler, Klein, Rollie, Pacheco, Hartsfield, & Wothke, in press).

Although these psychosocial functioning outcome analyses provided convincing evidence of the intervention's 12-month effectiveness, it is equally important to assess any *sustained effects* the FEI has. Intervention programs can often demonstrate success in improving psychosocial functioning while youths are involved in the program or for a short period afterwards. Substantially fewer programs can document continued beneficial effects for periods longer than one year post-intervention (University of Colorado Center for the Study and Prevention of Violence, 1999). This is the purpose of the analyses we report. Depending on the year youths entered the project, we completed up to three annual reinterviews with them following their initial assessment. The results of the long-term psychosocial functioning analyses provide evidence in support of the *sustained effect* of the FEI among youths completing the FEI.

THE YOUTH SUPPORT PROJECT

As discussed in more detail elsewhere, the YSP implemented a 10-week systems-oriented and structural approach to family preservation: a home-based Family Empowerment Intervention (FEI) (Cervenka, Dembo, & Brown, 1996; Dembo, Shemwell, Guida, Schmeidler, Pacheco & Seeberger, 1998). Families involved in the project were randomly assigned to one of two groups: the Extended Services Intervention (ESI) or the Family Empowerment Intervention (FEI) group. ESI group families received monthly phone contacts from project Research Assistants (RAs), and FEI group families received personal in-home visits from project Field Consultants (FCs). Project FCs visited families to work on the following goals: (1) restore the family hierarchy (parents, children, etc.); (2) restructure boundaries between parents and children; (3) encourage parents to take greater responsibility for family functioning; (4) increase family structure through implementation of rules and consequences; (5) enhance parenting skills; (6) have parents set limits, expectations, and rules that increase the likelihood the target youth's behavior will improve; (7) improve communication skills among all family members; (8) improve problem-solving skills, particularly in the target youth; and (9) where needed, connect the family to other systems (e.g., school, church, community activities). It was expected that empowering parents will result in improvements in the target youth's behavior and psychosocial functioning–including reduced recidivism.

FEI families were expected to participate in three, one-hour family meetings per week for approximately ten weeks. All household members (i.e., individuals living under the same roof as the target youth) were expected to participate in these meetings. Both FEI and ESI families had twenty-four hour a day, seven days a week access to YSP staff, and to information on various community resources via a project developed agency and services resource file. YSP staff provided families with information about different community agencies and assisted them in obtaining appropriate referrals to meet their needs.

A distinctive feature of this intervention is that the families were served by Field Consultants, who are not trained therapists–although they were trained by, and perform their work under the direction of, licensed clinicians. The choice of paraprofessionals was based on a cost effectiveness argument and is supported by experimental research indicating that, at least for some treatments, paraprofessionals produce outcomes that are better than those under control conditions, and similar to those involving professional therapists (Christensen & Jacobson, 1994; Weisz, Weiss, Han, Granger, & Morton, 1995). Further, by requiring less previous therapy training, the FEI, if proven effective, is expected to be highly attractive to agencies providing services to juvenile offenders, which often operate with financial constraints.

Youths processed at the Hillsborough County Juvenile Assessment Center (JAC) (Dembo & Brown, 1994) who were arrested on misdemeanor or felony charges were sampled for inclusion in the project. When openings occurred on the Field Consultants' case loads, a listing of recently arrested youths was drawn. A cross-tabulation of these cases was completed in regard to their gender and race/ethnicity (African-American, Latino, and Anglo), and equal numbers of youths in each of these six cells were randomly selected to process for enrollment in the Youth Support Project. This procedure and large sample size provided good representation of African-American, Latino, and Anglo youths of both sexes and their families in the study. Of the 315 youths entering the YSP between September 1, 1994, and January 31, 1998, the data in this article include 278 (88%) youths who completed at least one follow-up interview.

METHOD

Initial and Follow-Up Interviews

Initial interviews were completed with 315 youths processed at the Hillsborough County Juvenile Assessment Center from September 1, 1994, through January 31, 1998. Each youth was paid $10.00 for completing the one and one-half to two-hour initial interview. Depending on the year youths entered the project, up to three annual follow-up interviews were completed as follows:

Period of Initial Interview (Year 1)	n	Follow-Up Interviews Sought
September 1, 1994-January 31, 1996	120	Year 2, Year 3, Year 4
February 1, 1996-January 31, 1997	80	Year 2, Year 3
February 1, 1997-January 31, 1998	115	Year 2
Total:	315	

Table 1 presents the Year 2, Year 3 and Year 4 follow-up interview outcomes. As can be seen, overall completion rates of 86.3%, 85.0% and 75.8% were achieved for the Year 2, Year 3 and Year 4 interviews, respectively. The follow-up interviews averaged one and one-half hours. Each youth was paid $20.00 for a completed follow-up interview. Importantly, we had a low refusal rate for each follow-up interview. If we exclude youths who moved out of state (who were not routinely followed-up) and youths who could not be located, we achieved net reinterview success rates of 93.5%, 93.4%, and 91% for the Year 2, Year 3, and Year 4 interviews, respectively. There were no significant differences in the reinterview results for FEI and ESI youths. Ninety-four percent of the Year 2 interviews, 93 percent of the Year 3 interviews, and 97 percent of the Year 4 interviews were completed within 120 days following the anniversary of their preceding interview.

For each youth, the last available observation was used in the analysis, as the best measure of long-term outcome. The data set used in the analyses consisted of Year 2 interview data on 107 youths, Year 3 interview data on 81 youths, and Year 4 interview data on 90 youths. The youths were interviewed in a variety of settings at each interview wave. A majority of youths were interviewed at home or in another community location. However, other youths were interviewed in Florida Department of Juvenile Justice residential commitment programs, county jails, juvenile detention centers, or in another type of secure program such as prison.

Comparison of the 278 Reinterviewed Youths with the Other Youths in the Study

A discriminant analysis (Bennett & Bowers, 1976; Klecka, 1980) was performed comparing the 278 reinterviewees, for whom we had initial interview and last interview follow-up interview data, with the other 37 youths in the study to learn if there were any important differences between the two groups. The two groups were compared in regard to their initial interview demographic characteristics (age, gender, ethnicity, race, living situation); family

Status	Year 2 (n = 315)	Year 3 (n = 200)	Year 4 (n = 120)
Completed	86.3%	85.0%	75.8%
Lost case	5.1%	6.0%	10.0%
Living out of state	2.5%	3.0%	6.7%
Refusal	6.0%	6.0%	7.5%
	99.9%	100.0%	100.0%

☐ **Table 1: Follow-Up Interview Results Among Eligible Youths**

members' alcohol, other drug abuse, or mental health problems, and family member contact with the justice system; lifetime self-reported history of physical abuse, sexual victimization, and frequency of marijuana/hashish use in blunt and non-blunt form, hallucinogen, and cocaine use; lifetime history of referrals to juvenile court on delinquency charges or for dependency (i.e., physical abuse, sexual exploitation/victimization, neglect); lifetime reported treatment for a substance abuse or mental health problem, and the lag between the youths' grade level and their chronological age; friends' substance use and involvement with the justice system; self-reported delinquency in the year prior to initial interview and reported frequency of getting drunk or very high on alcohol in the past year; RIAH® hair test results for marijuana, cocaine, and opiates; arrest charges upon entering the juvenile assessment center (i.e., violence offenses, property offenses, drug offenses, or public disorder misdemeanors); emotional/psychological functioning as measured by the SCL-90-R (Derogatis, 1983); being a diversion (minor offender) or more serious offender case; and assignment to the ESI or FEI group. The results indicated that, overall, the two groups were not significantly different from one another on these variables (chi-squared test of Wilks' lambda = 44.59, df = 32, p = n.s.). The two groups were significantly different from one another on only three of the comparison variables: (1) African-American youths were more likely to be included among the reinterviews (F = 5.41, df = 1,313, p = .021); (2) youths with positive hair test results for marijuana were less likely to be included in the reinterviews (F = 4.15, df = 1,313, p = .042); and (3) youths charged with drug offenses upon entering the assessment center were less likely to be included in the reinterviews (F = 4.74, df = 1,313, p = .030). None of these relationships were significant by the .05/32 = .002 Bonferroni inequality criterion that takes the account of the number of predictors.

Demographic, Educational, and Treatment History Description of the Youths

As Table 2 shows, most youths were male (56%) and averaged 14.5 years of age. Fifty-six percent of the youths were Anglo; 41 percent were African-American. Twenty-six percent of the youths were Latino. Seventeen percent of the youths indicated they lived with both their biological parents; an additional 64 percent indicated they resided with either their mother only (51%), mother and another adult (5%), or mother and stepfather (8%). Information on the occupational status of the household chief wage earner or other sources of household income (derived from Fishburne, Abelson, & Cisin, 1980), a measure of socioeconomic status, highlighted the low to moderate SES of the youths' families. Eleven percent of the chief wage earners held an

☐ *Table 2: Demographic, Educational, and Treatment History Description of the Youths in the Study*

Race	n	%		Age	n	%
African-American	115	41%		11	13	5%
Native American/Indian	1	<1%		12	12	4%
Oriental	1	<1%		13	45	16%
Anglo	156	56%		14	69	25%
Other	5	2%		15	60	22%
Total	278	99%		16	39	14%
				17	39	14%
				18	1	<1%
				Total	278	100%
				Mean =	14.54	
				Standard deviation =	1.60	

Sex	n	%		Ethnicity	n	%
Male	155	56%		Latino	72	26%
Female	123	44%		Non-Latino	206	74%
Total	278	100%		Total	278	100%

Occupational Status/Income Source of Household Head	n	%		Living Situation	n	%
Executive, Administrative, and Managerial Occupations/ Professional Specialty Occupations	31	11%		Biological Parents	47	17%
				Father	7	3%
				Father and Stepmother	6	2%
Technical, Sales, Administrative Support Occupations	37	13%		Mother	142	51%
				Mother and Stepfather	21	8%
Skilled Occupations	13	5%		Mother and Other Adult	14	5%
Unskilled, Semiskilled, and Low or Moderate Skilled Service Occupations	104	37%		Grandmother/Grandfather	13	5%
				Aunt	7	3%
Public Assistance/Other Public Support	23	8%		Guardian	8	3%
				Boyfriend	1	<1%
No Information	70	25%		Other	11	4%
Total	278	99%		Total	276	101%

Repeated a Grade	n	%		Currently in School	n	%
Yes	140	50%		Yes	245	88%
No	138	50%		No	33	12%
Total	278	100%		Total	278	100%

Placed in a Special Education Class	n	%		Lag Between Grade and Chronological Age	n	%
Yes	123	44%		2 Grades Above	2	1%
No	153	55%		1 Grade Above	7	3%
No Information	2	1%		At Grade Level	88	32%
Total	278	100%		1 Grade Below	122	44%
				2 Grades Below	39	14%
				3 Grades Below	11	4%
				4 Grades Below	1	<1%
				No Information	8	3%
				Total	278	101%

Mental Health Treatment History	n	%		Substance Abuse Treatment History	n	%
Never	219	79%		Never	259	93%
Previously	44	16%		Previously	12	4%
Currently	11	4%		Currently	3	1%
Refused to Answer	2	1%		Refused to Answer	2	1%
No Information	2	1%		No Information	2	1%
Total	278	101%		Total	278	100%

executive, administrative/managerial, or professional specialty type position; in contrast, 37 percent held unskilled, semiskilled, or low/moderate skilled service occupations; and eight percent of the youths' households were supported by public funds. Twenty-five percent of the cases had missing or uncodable information on this variable.

Although most of the youths (88%) were still attending school, sizable proportions of them were experiencing educational problems. For example, 44 percent of the youths indicated they had been placed in a special educational program (e.g., Emotionally Handicapped, Specific Learning Disability), and 50 percent noted they had repeated a grade in school. Relatedly, most youths (62%) lagged one or more grade levels behind the grade level that would be expected based on their chronological age. Few youths reported current (4%) or previous (16%) mental health treatment. Even fewer youths reported current (1%) or previous (4%) substance abuse treatment.

Arrest Charges upon Entering JAC

Almost all the youths entered JAC as a result of being taken into custody on one or more felony or misdemeanor charges. Many of the youths were charged with felony property offenses (52%) (especially burglary, grand larceny, or auto theft) or misdemeanor property charges (e.g., retail theft) (41%). Relatively few youths were arrested on charges of felony (17%) or misdemeanor violence (2%), on felony (6%) or misdemeanor drug charges (4%), or on public disorder misdemeanors (8%).

Referral History

Information obtained from the Florida Department of Juvenile Justice (DJJ) indicated 33 percent of the youths had been referred to juvenile court at least once for misdemeanor property offenses, 26 percent for felony property offenses, 22 percent for misdemeanor violence offenses, 18 percent for felony violence offenses, and 16 percent for misdemeanor public disorder offenses. Appendix A gives a detailed list of the various referral categories. As Table 3 shows, the youths were victims as well as offenders; 18 percent had been referred to juvenile court for being physically abused and 17 percent for being neglected.

A factor analysis was completed on the delinquency referral variables to see how they clustered. The initial principal components analysis identified two factors with eigenvalues greater than 1.0, 2.28, and 1.38, which were rotated using varimax criteria for factor clarity. Table 4 shows the loadings of the two factors identified in these data: (1) violence, property, and public disorder of-

☐ Table 3: Youths' History at Time of Initial Interview

Reason for Referral	Frequency of Referral to Florida Department of Juvenile Justice (% of youths) (n = 278)	
	Referred 1 or more times	Referred 4 or more times
Felony Property Offenses	26%	6%
Felony Violence Offenses	18%	0%
Felony Drug Offenses	4%	0%
Misdemeanor Property Offenses	33%	8%
Misdemeanor Violence Offenses	22%	2%
Misdemeanor Public Disorder Offenses	16%	2%
Misdemeanor Drug Offenses	6%	<1%
Status Offenses	1%	0%
Victim of Neglect	17%	1%
Victim of Mental Injury	1%	0%
Victim of Sexual Abuse/Exploitation	7%	0%
Victim of Physical Abuse	18%	0%

☐ Table 4: Loading of the Delinquency Referral History Variables on the Two Varimax Factors (n = 278) (Decimal points omitted)

Referral History Variables	Factor 1: Violence, Property and Public Disorder Offenses	Factor 2: Drug Offenses
Felony Property Offenses	71	18
Felony Violence Offenses	54	05
Felony Drug Offenses	03	87
Misdemeanor Property Offenses	71	12
Misdemeanor Violence Offenses	58	−05
Misdemeanor Public Disorder Offenses	70	01
Misdemeanor Drug Offenses	11	85
Rotation Sums of Squared Loadings	2.12	1.54
Percent of Variance Explained	30.30	22.01

fenses and (2) drug offenses. Based on these results, regression factor scores were calculated (Kim & Mueller, 1978). The higher the score on each factor, the more frequent the referrals.

Family Problem Characteristics

The youths tend to come from families who have experienced a number of difficulties in psychosocial functioning. Thirty-seven percent of the youths reported that at least one member of their family or household family, besides themselves, had an alcohol abuse problem; 25 percent noted a family or household family member had another drug abuse problem (most frequently marijuana/hashish); and 23 percent indicated a family or household member had experienced an emotional or mental health problem. In addition, many members of the youths' families or household families have had experience with the juvenile or adult justice systems. Sixty-six percent of the youths claimed at least one member of their family or household family, besides themselves, had been arrested, and from 44 percent to 57 percent reported that a member of their family/household family had been held in jail/detention (57%), adjudicated delinquent or convicted of a crime (46%), or put on community control or probation (44%). Further, 33 percent of the youths noted at least one family member or household family member had been sent to a training school or prison.

A principal components analysis was completed on the family member alcohol abuse, other drug abuse, emotional/mental health problem and contact with the justice system variables to see how they clustered. Two principal components had eigenvalues above 1.0, 3.89, and 1.39, which were rotated using varimax criteria for factor clarity. Table 5 shows the two factors that were identified in these data: (1) family member involvement with the justice system and (2) family member alcohol, other drug abuse, or mental health problems. Based on these results, summary regression factor scores (Kim & Mueller, 1978) were created for further analyses. For each factor, higher scores indicate more family problems.

Friends' Substance Use and Involvement with the Police or Courts

As Table 6 shows, 55 percent of the youths noted that one or more of their close friends had used alcohol, 50 percent marijuana/hashish, and 13 percent claimed at least one close friend used a hallucinogen, during the year prior to their initial interview. Under 10 percent noted a friend's use of cocaine, inhalants, heroin, or the nonmedical use of stimulants, analgesics, tranquilizers, or sedatives. In addition, large proportions of the youths' close friends had some

☐ **Table 5: Loading of Family Member Alcohol, Other Drug,
Mental Health Problem, and Justice System Contact
Variables on the Two Varimax Factors (n = 278)***
(Decimal points omitted)

Variables	Factor 1: Involvement with the Justice System	Factor 2: Alcohol, Other Drug, and Mental Health Problems
Youth reporting any family/household member:		
Had an alcohol abuse problem	06	70
Had another drug abuse problem	18	78
Had an emotional/mental health problem	05	65
Had been arrested	87	07
Had been held in jail or detention	89	07
Had been adjudicated delinquent or convicted of a crime	88	13
Had been placed on community control or probation	88	08
Had been sent to a training school or prison	74	22
Rotation Sums of Squared Loadings	3.68	1.59
Percent of variance explained	46.04	19.92

*For each variable, missing values are replaced by the variable mean.

type of contact with the legal system. Sixty-six percent of the youths claimed at least one of their close friends had been arrested, and from 43 percent to 51 percent indicated that one or more of their close friends had been held in jail or detention (51%), adjudicated delinquent or convicted of a crime (45%), or been put on community control or probation (43%). In addition, 14 percent of the youths reported that at least one of their close friends had been sent to a training school or prison.

A principal components analysis was completed on the friends' use of alcohol, marijuana/ hashish, cocaine and hallucinogens, and justice system contact variables as a data reduction technique and to see how they clustered. (Low frequency behaviors, such as friends' use of heroin, were excluded from this factor analysis.) Two principal components had eigenvalues above 1.0, 4.22, and 1.46, which were rotated using varimax criteria for factor clarity. As Table 7 shows, two factors were identified in the data: (1) friends' involvement with the justice system (short of being sent to a training school or prison) and (2) friends' drug use and being sent to a training school or prison. Based on

☐ **Table 6: Friends' Prevalence of Alcohol/Other Drug Use and Involvement with the Police or Courts**

Characteristic	n	%
Youths reporting any close friend used any of the following substances in the past year*:		
Alcohol	267	55%
Marijuana/hashish	267	50%
Inhalants	268	6%
Hallucinogens	268	13%
Cocaine	268	7%
Heroin	267	3%
Nonmedical use of:		
Stimulants	268	5%
Sedatives	268	4%
Tranquilizers	268	4%
Analgesics	268	6%
Youths reporting any close friend had been:		
Arrested	267	66%
Held in jail or detention	267	51%
Adjudicated delinquent or convicted of a crime	267	45%
Placed on community control or probation	267	43%
Sent to a training school or prison	267	14%

* Responses ranged as follows: used in the past week = 5, used in the past month = 4, used in the past six months = 3, used in the past twelve months = 2, not used = 1.

these results, regression factor scores (Kim & Mueller, 1978) were created for each varimax factor as a summary measure for further analysis. Higher scores indicated more reported friends' involvement with the justice system and drug use.

Physical Abuse

Drawing upon the work of Straus and his associates (Straus, 1979, 1983; Straus, Gelles, & Steinmetz, 1980), we used six items designed to determine the youths' physical abuse experiences. The youths were asked whether they had ever: (1) been beaten or *really* hurt by being hit (but not with anything) (25%); (2) been beaten or hit with a whip, strap, or belt (39%); (3) been beaten or hit with something "hard" (like a club or stick) (16%); (4) been shot with a gun, injured with a knife, or had some other "weapon" used against them (7%); (5) been hurt badly enough to require (need) a doctor or bandages or other

☐ **Table 7: Loading of Close Friends' Alcohol/Other Drug Use, and Justice System Contact Variables on the Two Varimax Factors (n = 278)***
(Decimal points omitted)

Variables	Factor 1: Involvement with the Justice System	Factor 2: Drug Use
Youths reporting any close friend used any of the following substances in the past year:		
Alcohol	29	74
Marijuana/hashish	28	74
Hallucinogens	09	70
Cocaine	01	66
Youths reporting any close friend had ever been:		
Arrested	87	13
Held in jail or detention	88	15
Adjudicated delinquent or convicted of a crime	87	26
Placed on community control or probation	85	20
Sent to a training school or prison	38	44
Rotation Sums of Squared Loadings	3.31	2.36
Percent of variance explained	36.82	26.22

* For each variable, missing values are replaced by the variable mean.

medical treatment (11%); and (6) spent time in a hospital because they were physically injured (5%). Normative data on this behavior are difficult to obtain. However, available information from the 1995 national survey on family violence (Straus, Hamby, Finkelhor, Moore, & Runyan, 1998) found parent-to-child violence prevalence rates for being hit with something (5%), beaten up (0.6%), or threatened with a knife or gun (0.1%) that were lower than those reported by the youths we interviewed. The youths we studied reported physical abuse experiences that are consistent with the rates of such experiences reported by juveniles involved in the Tampa longitudinal study of juvenile detainees (Dembo, Williams, & Schmeidler, 1998).

We probed the validity of the youths' self-reports of physical abuse by determining whether youths with a record of having been referred to the Department of Health and Rehabilitative Services (HRS) on one or more occasions for physical abuse reported physical abuse in the interview. Sixty-eight percent of such youths reported experiencing one or more of the six specific modes of physical harm. As a data reduction procedure (Kim & Mueller, 1978), a principal components analysis was undertaken on the six physical abuse modes. Two principal components with eigenvalues greater than 1.0, 2.50, and 1.04 were identified in these data. These clusters were varimax rotated for factor clarity. Table 8 displays the two factors that were identified in these data: (1) serious physical harm and (2) been beaten or hit. On the basis of these results, regression factor scores were created (Kim & Mueller, 1978). For each factor, higher scores indicated more different modes of physical harm claimed.

Sexual Victimization

Drawing upon the work of Finkelhor (1979), the youths were asked a number of the questions regarding their sexual experience. Each youth was asked if he or she ever had a sexual experience such as showing sex organs, touching sex organs, or intercourse. Respondents answering "yes" to this question were asked how many of these experiences they had had. Consistent with Finkelhor's (1979) operational definition, all youths who were 13 years of age or younger at the time of a sexual experience with a person over the age of 18 were considered to have been sexually victimized. In addition, youths who had a sexual experience at any age and who reported they were forced or threatened, reacted to the experience with fear or shock, or had this experience with their parent,

---

☐ **Table 8: Loading of Self-Reported Physical Abuse Items**
on the Two Varimax Components (n = 278)*
(Decimal points omitted)

Item	Factor 1: Serious Physical Harm	Factor 2: Beaten or Hit
Been beaten or *really* hurt by being hit (but not with anything)	20	77
Been beaten or hit with a whip, strap, or belt	04	82
Been beaten or hit with something "hard" (like a club or stick)	54	37
Been shot with a gun, injured with a knife, or had some other "weapon" used against you	78	08
Been hurt badly enough by an adult to require (need) a doctor or bandages or other medical treatment	75	33
Spent time in the hospital because you were physically injured by an adult	72	−01
Rotation Sums of Squared Loadings:	2.02	1.51
Percent of variance explained:	33.7	25.2

*For each variable, missing values are replaced by the variable mean.

stepparent, or grandparent were also considered to have been sexually victimized. In line with this operational definition, consenting relationships between youths aged 14 to 17 years and an adult would not be classified as sexual abuse. Twenty-five percent of the youths had been sexually victimized at least once in their lives (35% of the females and 18% of the males: chi square = 11.00, df = 1, p < .001). This rate of sexual victimization is comparable to that Mouzakitis (1981) found among the Arkansas training school girls he studied. It is also similar to the rate reported by youths involved in the Tampa longitudinal study of juvenile detainees (Dembo, Williams, & Schmeidler, 1998).

Self-Reported Alcohol and Illicit Drug Use Prior to Initial Interview

A number of questions on substance use were adopted from the National Household Survey on Drug Abuse to determine the youths' use of various categories of substances: tobacco, alcohol, marijuana/hashish (in non-blunt form), marijuana in blunt form, inhalants, hallucinogens, cocaine, heroin and the nonmedical use of barbiturates and other sedatives, tranquilizers, stimulants, and analgesics. The youths' use of tobacco is not considered in this article.

Alcohol Use

The survey questions regarding the youths' alcohol use probed their age of first use, recency of use, the number of days used in the past month, and the number of times the youths got very high or drunk on alcohol in the past year. Our analysis of the alcohol use data focused on the youths' responses to the question probing the number of times in the 12 months prior to their initial interviews they reported being very high or drunk on alcohol. As the results shown in Table 9 indicate, 19 percent of the youths reported they had gotten very high or drunk on alcohol 12 or more days in the 12 months preceding their initial interview.

Lifetime Frequency of Illicit Drug Use

Questions concerning the youths' illicit drug use or nonmedical use of psychotherapeutic drugs probed their age of first use, lifetime frequency of use, and recency of use. The present analyses focus on the youths' reported lifetime frequency of drug use, presented in Table 10a. Over half (55%) of the youths used marijuana in non-blunt form and almost as many (50%) in blunt form. The claimed use of hallucinogens (14%) and cocaine (13%) was at much

☐ **Table 9: How Many Times Reported Getting Very High or Drunk on Alcohol**

Frequency	In Year Before Initial Interview		Last Available Observation	
	n	%	n	%
None	154	55%	132	48%
1 or 2 days	31	11%	45	16%
3 to 5 days	17	6%	32	12%
Every other month or so (or 6 to 11 days)	24	9%	16	6%
1 to 2 times a month (or 12 to 24 days a year)	17	6%	20	7%
Several times a month (or 25 to 51 days a year)	9	3%	13	5%
About 1 or 2 days a week	13	5%	10	4%
Almost daily or 3 to 6 days a week	10	4%	5	2%
Daily	3	1%	5	2%
Total	278	100%	278	102%

lower rates. No other drug was used by more than 10 percent of the youths. Seventeen percent of the youths claimed to have used marijuana/hashish in non-blunt form, and 11 percent marijuana in blunt form, 100 or more times in their lives. Little use of other drugs was claimed. Since the reported lifetime frequency of marijuana/hashish use in non-blunt form (e.g., reefers) and in blunt form was strongly associated ($r = .693$, $n = 278$, $p < .001$), a composite index of the youths' use of marijuana/hashish was created, summing standardized scores for these two variables, for use in subsequent analyses. The drug use lifetime prevalence rates shown in Table 10 are higher than those reported by the 12- to 17-year-old youths interviewed in the 1996 National Household Survey on Drug Abuse (Substance Abuse and Mental Health Services Administration, 1997) (given in parentheses): marijuana/hashish–55% (vs. 17% in the NHSDA sample), hallucinogens–14% (vs. 6%), and cocaine–13% (vs. 2%).

Self-Reported Alcohol and Illicit Drug Use During the Follow-Up Period

Alcohol Use

As Table 9 indicates, 20 percent of the youths reported getting very high or drunk on alcohol 12 or more days during the year preceding their last follow-up interview. This rate is similar to the rate reported by the youths at the time of their initial interviews.

☐ **Table 10: The Youths' Reported Frequency of Drug Use**

a. Lifetime Prior to Initial Interview

Drug	Never used	Used 1-2 times	Used 3-5 times	Used 6-10 times	Used 11-49 times	Used 50-99 times	Used 100-199 times	Used 200+ times	Total (n = 277) or 278)
Marijuana/hashish (not blunts)	45%	8%	5%	5%	15%	4%	4%	13%	99%
Blunts	50%	12%	7%	7%	9%	4%	3%	8%	100%
Hallucinogens	86%	6%	2%	2%	3%	1%	-	-	100%
Cocaine	87%	6%	1%	1%	2%	1%	<1%	<1%	98%

b. In the Year Preceding the Last Available Observation

Drug	Never used	Used 1-2 times	Used 3-5 times	Used 6-10 times	Used 11-49 times	Used 50-99 times	Used 100-199 times	Used 200+ times	To-tal (n = 277) or 278)
Marijuana/hashish (including blunts)	39%	8%	5%	5%	6%	5%	9%	22%	99%
Hallucinogens	86%	8%	1%	2%	2%	<1%	-	<1%	99%
Cocaine	87%	4%	5%	1%	2%	<1%	-	1%	100%

Frequency of Illicit Drug Use

At the time of their last follow-up interviews, the youths also reported relatively high rates of marijuana/hashish use (including the use of blunts) in the past year, with 31 percent reporting use 100 or more times. Again, little use of the other categories of drugs probed was claimed (see Table 10b). Self-reported use of marijuana/hashish during the follow-up period was not corrected for time at risk. This variable was coded as a categorical variable, with each code referring to a range of values. Relatively few youths had time at risk small enough to increase their scores if they were in intermediate categories. Thus, such a refinement in scoring would not have had an appreciable effect on the analyses.

Hair Testing for Drug Use

An important part of the youths' interviews was obtaining hair specimens for analysis for recent drug use. About one-and-a-half inches of hair is collected across a finger and cut as close to the scalp as possible. The hair specimens were prepared for shipment following the established protocol of Psychemedics Corporation in Culver City, California, and were processed by them. Psychemedics technicians weigh them and evaluate any cosmetic damage to the hair by a staining process. Following this process, the hair samples are weighed and washed once for 15 minutes in isopropanol and three times for 30 minutes each in phosphate buffer at pH = 5.5. The hair is then converted into a liquid state by a patented digestion method. The resulting digested sample is assayed by radioimmunoassay (RIAH®) for presence of specific drugs. Psychemedics performed RIAH® testing of the hair samples for the past 90 days use of the following substances: cocaine, opiates, PCP, methamphetamines, and marijuana. The cutoff for a positive for cocaine and methamphetamines was 5 ng/10 mg hair; for PCP it was 3 ng/10 mg of hair; for opiates it was 2 ng/10 mg of hair; for marijuana it was 10 pg carboxy–THC equivalents/10 mg of hair. (In a few cases where hair was not available, fingernail samples were collected, analyzed, and included in the hair test results.)

In the case of cocaine and opiates, the antibody used in the radioimmunoassay does not produce any false positive results. With the marijuana radioimmunoassay, between 5 to 10 percent of positive results may be false positives as a result of hair matrix effects near the cutoff level of the assay. False negatives are determined by the values of the cutoff level. For cocaine, individuals using less than one to three lines of cocaine per month are reported as negative. For opiates, individuals using less than two bags of heroin per week are scored as negative. For marijuana, because of its 100,000 lower concentration in hair than cocaine, it appears that only the heavy and moderate, but not the light user, is identified by the hair assay. The exact clinical definitions of these categories of use have not been established to date (Baumgartner & Hill, 1996).

Initial Interview Hair Test Results

As Table 11 shows, 44 percent of the youths tested were positive on one or more of the five drugs at their initial interviews. Overall, 38 percent of the youths were positive on marijuana, and 22 percent were positive on cocaine.

Last Follow-Up Interview Hair Test Results

Hair specimens were collected from 235 youths at the time of their last follow-up interviews. Most non-collected samples involved youths who were interviewed in long-term secure facilities; a few youths refused to provide a hair sample. As Table 11 shows, the last observation hair test results reflected a 28 percentage point increase in the marijuana positive rate and a 5 percent increase in the cocaine positive rate among the youths.

		☐ **Table 11: Hair Test Results (RIAH®)**		
	At Initial Interview		Last Available Observation	
Frequency	n	%	n	%
No Drug Positives	147	56%	80	29%
Positive for:				
Marijuana	90*	38%	141**	66%
Cocaine	59	22%	64	27%
Opiates	5	2%	5	2%
Methamphetamines	1	<1%	9	4%
PCP	0	-	0	-
Number of Youths Providing Hair Samples	264		235	

*Based on 234 cases tested on all 5 drugs. Excludes 30 cases with samples of hair that were insufficient to test for marijuana.

**Based on 213 cases tested on all 5 drugs. Excludes 22 cases with samples of hair that were insufficient to test for marijuana.

Self-Reported Delinquent Behavior

Drawing upon the work of Elliott, Ageton, Huizinga, Knowles, and Canter (1983), we probed the youths' delinquent behavior in the year prior to their initial interviews by asking how many times they engaged in 23 delinquent behaviors. In addition, as a check, youths noting they had engaged in a given act 10 or more times were asked to indicate how often they participated in this behavior (once a month, once every two or three weeks, once a week, two to three times a week, once a day, or two to three times a day). In addition, for each of the 23 delinquent behaviors in which the youth claimed to have engaged, he/she was asked the age during which the act first occurred.

Based on the youths' claimed frequency of participation in the various delinquent acts, we developed the following four summary indices of the youngsters delinquent involvement used by Elliott and his associates (1983):

- General Theft: stole a motor vehicle, stole something worth more than $50, bought stolen goods, stole something worth less than $5, stole something worth between $5 and $50, broke into a building or vehicle, joyriding.
- Crimes Against Persons: aggravated assault, gang fights, hit a teacher, hit a parent, hit a student, sexual assault, strong-armed students, strong-armed teachers, strong-armed others.

- Index crimes: aggravated assault, sexual assault, gang fights, stole a motor vehicle, stole something worth more than $50, broke into a building or vehicle, strong-armed students, strong-armed teachers, strong-armed others.
- Total Delinquency: the sum of the reported frequency of participation in the 23 delinquent activities.

In addition, we constructed a drug sales index for analyses as follows:

- Drug Sales: sold marijuana or hashish, sold cocaine or crack, sold other hard drugs, such as heroin or LSD.

Self-Reported Delinquency in the Year Prior to Initial Interview

Table 12 shows that the 278 youths reported relatively high rates of delinquency during the year prior to their interviews. As can be seen, high prevalence rates are reported for index offenses (58%), crimes against persons (72%), general theft (82%), drug sales (25%), and total delinquency (94%). Further, from 2 percent to 16 percent of the youths reported engaging in the

---

☐ **Table 12: Self-Reported Delinquency (n = 278)**

Frequency in Year Before Initial Interview

Index/Behavior*	0	1-4	5-29	30-54	55-99	100-199	200+	Total
Index offenses	42%	32%	17%	4%	2%	2%	<1%	99%
Crimes against persons	28%	37%	25%	4%	3%	2%	1%	100%
General theft	18%	37%	27%	8%	4%	4%	2%	100%
Drug sales	75%	10%	7%	2%	<1%	1%	4%	99%
Total delinquency	6%	27%	37%	9%	5%	5%	11%	100%

Frequency in Year Before Last Observation

Index/Behavior*	0	1-4	5-29	30-54	55-99	100-199	200+	Total
Index offenses	67%	19%	9%	2%	2%	<1%	<1%	99%
Crimes against persons	58%	24%	13%	1%	1%	1%	1%	98%
General theft	56%	20%	15%	2%	1%	3%	2%	99%
Drug sales	72%	6%	8%	2%	1%	4%	7%	100%
Total delinquency	33%	21%	20%	5%	2%	5%	13%	99%

*The construction of these indexes is discussed in the text.

offenses represented by the various scales 100 times or more–some reported many hundreds of offenses.

As can be seen in Table 12, the range of responses to the items comprising the five self-reported delinquency scales was large, ranging from no activity to hundreds (and in a few cases thousands). Raw numbers of offenses do form an interval scale, which might be useful if one were predicting crime rates for populations. However, the difference between no offense and one offense is not the same as the difference between 99 and 100 offenses in terms of involvement. Thus, analysis of the frequency data as an interval scale was not appropriate as a measure of involvement in delinquency/crime. A transformation was employed so that equal intervals on the transformed scale would represent equal differences in involvement. We interpreted the differences between 1 and 10, 10 and 100, and 100 and 1000 offenses as being comparable. Accordingly, we log transformed the numbers of offenses for each scale to the base 10.

For any base, logarithms exist for all positive numbers. The choice of base does not matter, if the logarithms are analyzed by a statistical procedure invariant under linear transformation, such as analysis of variance, multiple regression, discriminant analysis, or factor analysis. However, regardless of the base, the logarithm of zero does not exist. Some other method must be employed to determine the score assigned to no offenses. For any base, zero is the logarithm of the value one, and one is the logarithm of the base. If the difference from "base" offenses (10 in this study) to one offense is assigned the difference in logarithm scores of one and zero, this provides a unit of measurement for assigning a score even lower than zero–a negative number–to no offenses. In this study a score of minus one was assigned. This evaluates the difference between no offense and one offense as equal in importance as the difference between 1 offense and 10, or 10 offenses and 100.

Self-Reported Delinquency During the Follow-Up Period

At their last follow-up interviews, the youths reported lower prevalence rates of engaging in the offenses summarized by the four of the five scales (index offenses, 33%; crimes against persons, 42%; general theft, 44%; and total delinquency, 67%). However, the prevalence rate for drug sales increased to 28 percent. From < 1 percent to 18 percent of the 278 youths claimed to have engaged in the offenses represented by the various scales 100 or more times since their initial interviews–with some youths reporting many hundreds of delinquent acts (see Table 12).

The scoring of the self-reported delinquency follow-up data is complicated by the difference in time at risk. For every subject, time at risk could be ideally defined as the number of days in the community not in a secure facility. However, it was not feasible to determine this. The variable used in this study to represent the days at risk was the number of days between the last completed interview and the interview before it times the proportion of days in the community in the 365 days following the preceding interview. If the last follow-up interview was on the anniversary of the preceding interview, this would be the days at risk, ideally defined. Otherwise it is a good approximation. The days at risk is divided by 365 to yield years at risk.

Different years-at-risk corrections were applied to the cases of one or more offenses or of no offenses. To correct a positive number of offenses, before taking the logarithm, it was divided by years at risk. This gives the number of offenses that would have occurred at the same rate in 365 days at risk. If there was no offense, the assigned score–minus one in the study–was multiplied by the years at risk. This made the intensity of the negative score proportional to the length of time the person remained free of offenses.

Since correction for days at risk could inflate delinquent activities during the follow-up period, a frequency limit was established for each of the five self-reported delinquency scales: (1) general theft crimes, crimes against persons, and index crimes–1,095 per year (averaging to three offenses per day) for each scale, (2) drug sales–7,300 per year (an average of 20 drug sales per day), and (3) total delinquency–9,125 per year (an average of 25 delinquent acts per day). In all cases but one, youths reported frequencies of engaging in delinquent acts at levels below these limits. Paired sample t-tests on the transformed initial interview and last follow-up interview self-reported delinquency data on the five scales indicated statistically significant reductions in this behavior between the two time periods.

Validity of the Self-Reported Delinquency Data

In order to evaluate the accuracy of the youths' self-reported delinquency, we compared the total self-reported delinquency to the official recorded arrests in each follow-up period. It must be noted that if a youth had no official arrests, this does not invalidate reported delinquencies, since many delinquencies do not result in arrests. In contrast, if youths were arrested but reported no delinquencies, the validity of the denial of delinquency would be contradicted by the official record data. For the first follow-up period, 10 percent of the 133 youths with one or more arrests denied any delinquency. For the second and third follow-up periods, the comparable percentages were 20 percent of 65 arrested youths and 27 percent of 26 arrested youths. In contrast, among youths who were not arrested, the percentages who reported any delinquency were 57 percent, 58 percent, and 46 percent, respectively, in the three follow-up periods. These relatively low rates of denial of delinquency compared to the rates of admission of delinquency among youths who were not arrested suggest that most youths reported their delinquency accurately.

Emotional/Psychological Functioning

The SCL-90-R (Derogatis, 1983) was used to assess the youths' emotional/psychological functioning. The youths' replies to the items yielded T-scores on nine symptom dimensions: (1) somatization–distress arising from perceptions of bodily dysfunction; (2) obsessive-compulsive–symptoms that are closely identified with the standard clinical syndrome of the same name; (3) interpersonal sensitivity–feelings of personal inadequacy and inferiority, particularly in comparisons with others; (4) depression–a broad range of manifestations of clinical depression; (5) anxiety–a set of symptoms and signs that are associated clinically with high levels of manifest anxiety; (6) hostility–thoughts, feelings, or actions that are characteristic of the negative affect state of anger; (7) phobic anxiety–persistent fear of a specific person, place, object, or situation, characterized as irrational and disproportionate to the stimulus, leading to avoidance or escape behavior; (8) paranoid ideation–a disoriented mode of thinking; and (9) psychoticism–includes a range of items tapping functioning from mild interpersonal alienation to dramatic evidence of psychosis. The SCL-90-R has a long developmental history, has very good psychometric properties, and is widely used in clinical settings. It is easily administered (average test time is 12 to 15 minutes) and interpreted (Derogatis, 1983).

Emotional/Psychosocial Functioning at Initial Interview and Follow-Up Interviews

The T-score means for the nine SCL-90-R scales at initial interview (Year 1) and at Years 2, 3 and 4 are presented in Table 13. For each interview wave, comparison of the average T-score for the nine scales against the mean of 50 and standard deviation of 10 in the standardizing population indicated the T-scores for all nine scales were significantly lower than the norming population (adolescent non-patients) at the .001 level of significance.

Principal components analysis was completed on the SCL-90-R T-scores for the nine scale data at each interview wave to see how they clustered. Table 13 shows the one principal component with an eigenvalue greater than 1 resulting from the Year 1, Year 2, Year 3 and Year 4 analyses, together with the loadings of the various scales on these principal components. As can be seen, the loadings of the scales on the principal components were similar over time; for each principal component each of the scales loads highly and positively. Separate regression factor scores (Kim & Mueller, 1978) were created to sum-

□ **Table 13: SCL-90-R T-Score Means for the Nine Scales and Their Loading on the Main Principal Components, Year 1 to Year 4**

Scale	Year 1 (n = 278) T-Score Mean (x̄)	Loading*	Year 2 (n = 253) T-Score Mean (x̄)	Loading*	Year 3 (n = 159) T-Score Mean (x̄)	Loading*	Year 4 (n = 89) T-Score Mean (x̄)	Loading*
Somatization	45.4	79	44.4	75	44.2	67	45.6	72
Obsessive-compulsive	44.2	88	43.1	87	42.6	86	45.7	90
Interpersonal sensitivity	41.3	91	40.7	88	40.2	90	43.7	94
Depression	44.2	90	43.0	88	42.7	86	44.3	93
Anxiety	44.8	90	42.2	87	41.9	85	44.0	88
Hostility	46.2	79	45.2	76	44.1	78	46.7	85
Phobic anxiety	46.9	76	46.1	79	45.5	77	47.1	80
Paranoid ideation	45.8	87	45.0	86	44.2	89	46.5	88
Psychoticism	44.6	89	43.1	86	43.7	88	45.8	83
Eigenvalue:		6.61		6.34		6.24		6.70
Percent of Variance		73.5		70.5		69.3		74.5

* Decimal points omitted

marize these data for each principal component. Higher scores indicate more emotional/psychological problems.

Strategy of Analysis

The major focus of our analyses was to determine the impact of assignment to the FEI or ESI group on the youths' psychosocial functioning at last follow-up interview. Previous analyses (Dembo, Seeberger, Shemwell, Schmeidler, Klein, Rollie, Pacheco, Hartsfield, & Wothke, in press) highlighted the importance of completion of the FEI on the youths' 12-months post-intervention psychosocial outcomes. Hence, we were also interested in learning the longer-term impact of FEI completion on their psychosocial functioning. To examine this effect, we completed, for each psychosocial outcome variable, a regression analysis using all Year 1 predictor variables discussed in the next paragraph plus the Year 1 counterpart of the specific outcome variable being studied, to predict completion of the FEI. Separate stepwise regression or logistic regression analyses, with mean substitution for missing predictors, were performed on the youths': (1) emotional/psychological functioning at follow-up interview involving their SCL-90-R (Derogatis, 1983) data; (2) self-reported delinquency (general theft, crimes against persons, index crimes, drug sales, and total delinquency) during the follow-up period; (3) claimed frequency of getting very high or drunk on alcohol during the follow-up period; and (4) reported frequency of marijuana/hashish use during the follow-up period. In addition, separate stepwise logistic regression analyses were completed predicting the youths' recent (5) marijuana and (6) cocaine use at follow-up interview as indicated by their RIAH® hair test results.

Prior to conducting the regression analyses, a principal components analysis was completed on 23 of the youths' Year 1 psychosocial, offense history, and abuse-neglect history variables. Highly skewed variables with little variance (e.g., referral history for status offenses, substance abuse treatment history) were excluded from this analysis and did not contribute to the regression analyses. This analysis identified eight principal components with eigenvalues greater than 1.0 among these 23 predictor variables–accounting for 58 percent of the variance. Further, the commonalities of all variables were .36 to .73, except .29 for ever receiving mental health treatment reported at initial interview. These clusters were varimax rotated for factor clarity. Regression factor scores (Kim & Mueller, 1978) of these eight varimax rotated principal components, the youths' demographic characteristics (age, race, gender, ethnicity, and living situation), case type (whether the youth was a diversion or non-diversion case), and group assignment were included as predictor variables in the various regression analyses. Based on the loadings, presented in Appendix B, the varimax rotated factors were interpreted as reflecting drug use, delinquency history, psychosocial problems, drug offense history, property offenses at entering JAC, been hit or beaten, mental health treatment, and been seriously physically abused.

Principal components analysis (whether or not followed by rotation) is a standard treatment for potential collinearity problems among predictors (Draper & Smith, 1981). In addition, principal components regression averages out to some degree measurement error of predictors, if any, and thus diminishes error-in-variable problems. It also reduces the reduction in degrees of freedom due to covariates.

Our main interest in completing the multiple regression and logistic regression analyses was to control for the cumulative effect of various Year 1 predictor variables, including varimax rotated factors and demographics, before examining the effect on outcome of: (1) FEI (coded 1) or ESI (coded 0) group assignment, and (2) the variable reflecting completion of the FEI. (Another purpose in controlling for the Year 1 predictors was to reduce within-group variation in outcome associated with within-group differences in the Year 1 variables. The significance of the Year 1 predictors shows that this purpose was achieved for each outcome variable.) These predictors' unstandardized (b) and standardized (beta) regression coefficients and simple correlations (r) with the outcome variables are presented in the tables, but are not discussed in detail. This interest reflected the primary purpose of this study: to test the efficacy of FEI in comparison to ESI, which served as a less intensive control intervention. Therefore, a one-sided test was employed for the group assignment variable and the residualized variable comparing FEI completed and FEI non-completed youths. Thus, the Year 1 predictor variables were entered in a single step in each stepwise analysis, followed by the FEI or ESI group assignment variable and then the completion variable.

The test of significance of a beta is the same as the test of significance of the corresponding b, and also the test of significance of the partial correlation for that predictor, controlling for the effects of all other predictors. For the variables for group assignment and completion of the FEI, it is also the test of significance of R^2 change. If the analysis included the Year 1 predictors and group assignment but not the variable reflecting completion of the FEI, the interpretation of the beta for each Year 1 predictor would be that controlling for group assignment, in addition to all other Year 1 predictors, is equivalent to evaluating the effect of this predictor on the pooled results within the FEI and ESI groups, controlling for all other predictors. The analysis would be complicated by inclusion of a dichotomy distinguishing FEI completers from FEI non-completers and ESI youths. If FEI completion is substantially correlated with any Year 1 predictors, its inclusion in the analysis changes the betas for those predictors. To avoid this effect on the betas, a different variable was used for FEI completion in each analysis: the residual of the multiple regression predicting the FEI completion dichotomy using as predictors the Year 1 predictors for that dependent variable. This residual completion variable has no association with the other predictors, so it doesn't affect their betas. Using the residual rather than the original completion variable doesn't affect its own beta, because the effects of the other predictors are removed in any event. The one difference is that the correlation of the residual completion variable is the part correlation of the original completion predictor, controlling for the Year 1 predictors. A part correlation is an intermediate between a simple correlation and a partial correlation, removing the effects of the covariates from one of the variables but not the other; the partial correlation is always at least as large in magnitude as the part correlation.

RESULTS

Predicting Emotional/Psychological Functioning at Follow-Up Interview

The results of stepwise regression analysis predicting the youths' emotional/psychological functioning at last observation are shown in Table 14. In addition to the various Year 1 predictor variables discussed earlier, Year 1 emotional/psychological functioning was included as a predictor variable. The Year 1 predictors had $R^2 = 0.185$ (F = 3.95, df = 15,262, p < .001). In contrast, the R^2 change for the variable reflecting ESI or FEI group assignment was a nonsignificant 0.000. The residualized variable comparing FEI completed and FEI non-completed youths increased R^2 by 0.004, which was nonsignificant. Overall, all predictor variables account for 18.9 percent of the variance (F = 3.50, df = 17,260, p < .001).

Predicting Self-Reported Delinquency Since Initial Interview

Separate multiple regression analyses were conducted for each of the five last observation self-reported delinquency measures discussed earlier. In addition to the various Year 1 predictor variables, discussed earlier, that were included in the analyses, we included the Year 1 counterpart of the last observation delinquency measure being studied.

General Theft Offenses

Table 15 displays the results of a stepwise regression analysis predicting the youths' self-reported general theft offenses at last observation. The Year 1 predictors had $R^2 = 0.241$ (F = 5.43; df = 15,262; p < .001). The R^2 change (.003) associated with the FEI-ESI group assignment variable was quite low and nonsignificant. There was a low and nonsignificant R^2 change value (.002) associated with the residualized variable comparing FEI completed youths and FEI non-completed youths. Overall, all the predictor variables accounted for 24.6 percent of the variance (F = 4.99; df = 17,260; p < .001).

Crimes Against Persons

Table 16 displays the results of a stepwise regression analysis predicting the youths' self-reported crimes against persons at last observation. The Year 1 predictors had $R^2 = 0.257$ (F = 6.04; df = 15,262; p < .001). The R^2 change (.000) associated with the FEI-ESI group assignment variable was quite low and nonsignificant. However, there was statistically significant R^2 change value (.008) associated with residualized variable comparing FEI completed youths and FEI non-completed youths. Compared to FEI non-completed

☐ **Table 14: Regression and Correlation Coefficients of Emotional/Psychological Functioning at Last Interview as Measured by the SCL-90-R (n = 278)[†]**

Variables	b	(beta)	r	R^2 change
Age	.088	.139**	.142**	
Race (Black)	−.048	.023	.041	
Gender (male)	.223	.109*	.109*	
Ethnicity (Hispanic)	−.204	−.088	−.070	
Living situation (living with mother)	.246	.121**	.087	
Case Type (Arbitration/JASP)	−.048	−.023	−.132**	
Emotional/Psychological Functioning at Initial Interview	.248	.245***	.335****	
Psychosocial, Offense, & Abuse-Neglect History Rotated Factors:				
Varimax Factor 1	.015	.015	.070	
Varimax Factor 2	.045	.045	.195***	
Varimax Factor 3	.062	.061	.104*	
Varimax Factor 4	−.049	−.048	.023	
Varimax Factor 5	.073	.072	.098	
Varimax Factor 6	−.009	−.009	−.009	
Varimax Factor 7	.009	.009	.016	
Varimax Factor 8	.139	.137**	.220****	0.185 (F = 3.95**** df = 15,262)
Group assignment (FEI)	.038	.019	.023	0.000 (F = 0.11 df = 1,261)
Residualized Variable comparing FEI completed vs. FEI non-completed cases	.194	.064	.064	0.004 (F = 1.326 df = 1,260)
Constant	−1.406			Overall R^2 = 0.189 F for R^2 = 3.56**** df = 17,260

[†]The variables used in this analysis reported in Tables 14 to 23 were coded as follows:

age: age in years at first interview;
race: non-Black (mainly White) = 0, Black = 1;
gender: male = 1, female = 0;
ethnicity: non-Hispanic = 0, Hispanic = 1;
living situation: living with mother = 1, other living situation = 0;
case type: arbitration-JASP (diversion = 1), other cases = 0;
Psychosocial, offense history, and abuse history varimax factors: Higher scores indicate more characteristics/experiences loaded on the component.

Significance levels: For group assignment and for the residualized variable comparing FEI completed vs. FEI non-completed cases, significance levels are for a one-sided test. All other significance levels are for a two-tailed test:

*.10 > p > .05
**p < .05
***p < .01
****p < .001

☐ **Table 15: Regression and Correlation Coefficients of Self-Reported General Theft Offenses (n = 278)**

Variables	b	(beta)	r	R^2 change
Age	−.116	−.175***	−.112*	
Race (Black)	−.177	−.082	.066	
Gender (male)	.205	.096	.132**	
Ethnicity (Hispanic)	−.142	−.059	−.037	
Living situation (living with mother)	.115	.054	.039	
Case Type (Arbitration/JASP)	−.163	−.075	−.212****	
Self-Reported General Theft Offenses in Year Prior to Initial Interview	.241	.217***	.317****	
Psychosocial, Offense, & Abuse-Neglect History Rotated Factors:				
Varimax Factor 1	−.062	−.058	.041	
Varimax Factor 2	.133	.126**	.132**	
Varimax Factor 3	.191	.181***	.254****	
Varimax Factor 4	.119	.112*	.032	
Varimax Factor 5	.190	.180***	.257****	
Varimax Factor 6	.005	.005	.069	
Varimax Factor 7	.082	.078	.110*	
Varimax Factor 8	.057	.054	.063	0.241 (F = 5.43**** df = 15,262)
Group assignment (FEI)	−.111	−.053	−.105**	0.003 (F = 0.90 df = 1,261)
Residualized Variable comparing FEI completed vs. FEI non-completed cases	−.155	−.049	−.049	0.002 (F = 0.84 df = 1,260)
Constant	1.496			Overall R^2 = 0.246 F for R^2 = 4.99**** df = 17,260

youths, FEI completed youths reported committing fewer crimes against persons. Overall, all the predictor variables accounted for 26.5 percent of the variance (F = 5.52; df = 17,260; p < .001).

Index Crimes

Table 17 displays the results of a stepwise regression analysis predicting the youths' self-reported index crimes at last observation. The Year 1 predictor variables had R^2 = 0.227 (F = 5.13; df = 15,262; p < .001). The R^2 change (.000) associated with the FEI-ESI group assignment variable was low and nonsignificant.

☐ *Table 16: Regression and Correlation Coefficients of Self-Reported Crimes Against Persons (n = 278)*

Variables	b	(beta)	r	R² change
Age	−.117	−.199****	−.192***	
Race (Black)	.086	.045	.166***	
Gender (male)	.214	.113*	.131**	
Ethnicity (Hispanic)	−.026	−.012	−.058	
Living situation (living with mother)	−.084	−.045	−.033	
Case Type (Arbitration/JASP)	−.008	−.004	−.130**	
Self-Reported Crimes Against Persons in Year Prior to Initial Interview	.220	.218****	.352****	
Psychosocial, Offense & Abuse-Neglect History Rotated Factors:				
Varimax Factor 1	−.006	−.007	.011	
Varimax Factor 2	.079	.084	.085	
Varimax Factor 3	.089	.094	.158***	
Varimax Factor 4	.052	.055	−.043	
Varimax Factor 5	.196	.208****	.289****	
Varimax Factor 6	−.054	−.058	−.052	
Varimax Factor 7	.051	.054	.074	
Varimax Factor 8	.144	.153***	.200****	0.257 (F = 6.04 df = 15,262)
Group assignment (FEI)	.008	.004	−.058	0.000 (F = 0.01 df = 1,261)
Residualized Variable comparing FEI completed vs. FEI non-completed cases	−.256	−.091**	−.091*	0.008 (F = 2.91** df = 1,260)
Constant	1.274			Overall R²= 0.265 F for R² = 5.52**** df = 17,260

There was a nonsignificant R^2 change value of .003 associated with the residualized variable comparing FEI completed and FEI non-completed youths. Overall, all the predictor variables accounted for 23.0 percent of the variance (F = 4.57; df = 17,260; p < .001).

Drug Sales

Table 18 displays the results of a stepwise regression analysis predicting the youths' self-reported drug sales at last observation. The Year 1 predictor vari-

□ Table 17: Regression and Correlation Coefficients of Self-Reported Index Crimes (n = 278)

Variables	b	(beta)	r	R² change
Age	−.079	−.138**	−.061	
Race (Black)	−.178	−.096	.008	
Gender (male)	.115	.063	.155**	
Ethnicity (Hispanic)	−.014	−.006	.038	
Living situation (living with mother)	.046	.025	.021	
Case Type (Arbitration/JASP)	−.019	−.010	−.159***	
Self-Reported Index Crimes in Year Prior to Initial Interview	.287	.310****	.388****	
Psychosocial, Offense, & Abuse-Neglect History Rotated Factors:				
Varimax Factor 1	−.052	−.058	.094	
Varimax Factor 2	.053	.058	.077	
Varimax Factor 3	.180	.197***	.251****	
Varimax Factor 4	.100	.109*	.043	
Varimax Factor 5	.114	.125*	.228****	
Varimax Factor 6	.021	.023	.099	
Varimax Factor 7	.001	.001	.031	
Varimax Factor 8	.045	.049	.072	0.227 (F = 5.13**** df = 15,262)
Group assignment (FEI)	−.007	−.004	−.030	0.000 (F = 0.00 df = 1,261)
Residualized Variable comparing FEI completed vs. FEI non-completed cases	−.152	−.056	−.056	0.003 (F = 1.07 df = 1,260)
Constant	.754			Overall R² = 0.230 F for R² = 4.57**** df = 17,260

ables had $R^2 = 0.352$ (F = 9.48; df = 15,262; p < .001). The R^2 change associated with the FEI-ESI group assignment variable was .000. The R^2 change associated with the residualized variable comparing FEI completed and FEI non-completed youths (.009) was statistically significant (F = 3.51; df = 1,260; p < .05). Compared to FEI non-completed youths, FEI completed youths reported engaging in fewer drug sales. Overall, all the predictor variables accounted for 36.1 percent of the variance (F = 8.63; df = 17,260; p < .001).

☐ **Table 18:. Regression and Correlation Coefficients of Self-Reported Drug Sales (n = 278)**

Variables	b	(beta)	r	R^2 change
Age	−.051	−.064	.015	
Race (Black)	.091	.035	.085	
Gender (male)	.763	.298****	.390****	
Ethnicity (Hispanic)	.044	.015	.007	
Living situation (living with mother)	.229	.090*	.054	
Case Type (Arbitration/JASP)	−.035	−.014	−.249****	
Self-Reported Drug Sales in Year Prior to Initial Interview	.256	.206***	.422****	
Psychosocial, Offense, & Abuse-Neglect History Rotated Factors:				
Varimax Factor 1	.074	.058	.178***	
Varimax Factor 2	.004	.004	−.051	
Varimax Factor 3	.268	.211****	.306****	
Varimax Factor 4	.114	.090	.108*	
Varimax Factor 5	.196	.154***	.214****	
Varimax Factor 6	.033	.026	.071	
Varimax Factor 7	.096	.076	.099	
Varimax Factor 8	.095	.075	.143**	0.352 (F = 9.48**** df = 15,262)
Group assignment (FEI)	−.041	.051	−.064	0.000 (F = 0.10 df = 1,261)
Residualized Variable comparing FEI completed vs. FEI non-completed cases	−.350	−.093**	−.093*	0.009 (F = 3.51** df = 1,260)
Constant	.054			Overall R^2 = 0.361 F for R^2 = 8.63**** df = 17,260

Total Delinquency

Table 19 displays the results of a stepwise regression analysis predicting the youths' self-reported total delinquency at last observation. The Year 1 predictor variables had $R^2 = 0.332$ (F = 8.70; df = 15,262; p < .001). In addition, the R^2 change (.000) associated with the FEI-ESI group assignment variable was quite low and nonsignificant. There was a significant R^2 change value (.009) associated with the residualized variable comparing FEI completed and FEI

Variables	b	(beta)	r	R² change
Table 19: Regression and Correlation Coefficients of Self-Reported Total Delinquency (n = 278)				
Age	−.133	−.160***	−.086	
Race (Black)	.010	.004	.137**	
Gender (male)	.614	.229****	.261****	
Ethnicity (Hispanic)	.008	.003	−.019	
Living situation (living with mother)	.204	.077	.059	
Case Type (Arbitration/JASP)	.068	.025	−.216****	
Self-Reported Total Delinquency in Year Prior to Initial Interview	.257	.181**	.352****	
Psychosocial, Offense, & Abuse-Neglect History Rotated Factors:				
Varimax Factor 1	.020	.015	.084	
Varimax Factor 2	.090	.068	.040	
Varimax Factor 3	.358	.268****	.322****	
Varimax Factor 4	.192	.144**	.088	
Varimax Factor 5	.271	.203***	.283****	
Varimax Factor 6	−.059	−.044	.013	
Varimax Factor 7	.182	.136**	.153**	
Varimax Factor 8	.131	.098*	.146**	0.332 (F = 8.70**** df = 15,262)
Group assignment (FEI)	−.019	−.007	−.072	0.000 (F = 0.02 df = 15,261)
Residualized Variable comparing FEI completed vs. FEI non-completed cases	−.377	−.095**	−.095*	0.009 (F = 3.58** df = 1,260)
Constant	1.770			Overall R² = 0.341 F for R² = 7.93**** df = 17,260

non-completed youths. Compared to FEI non-completed youths, FEI completed youths reported engaging in less total delinquency. Overall, all the predictor variables accounted for 34.1 percent of the variance (F = 7.93; df = 17,260; p < .001).

Predicting Claimed Frequency of Getting Very High/Drunk on Alcohol Since Initial Interview

Table 20 shows the results of the stepwise regression analysis predicting the youths' reported frequency of getting very high or drunk on alcohol at last ob-

☐ **Table 20: Regression and Correlation Coefficients of Self-Reported Frequency of Getting Very High or Drunk on Alcohol (n = 278)**

Variables	b	(beta)	r	R^2 change
Age	.051	.039	.125**	
Race (Black)	−.601	−.143*	−.094	
Gender (male)	.518	.124**	.144**	
Ethnicity (Hispanic)	−.453	−.096	−.040	
Living situation (living with mother)	.194	.047	.030	
Case Type (Arbitration/JASP)	−.134	−.031	−.213****	
Self-Reported Frequency of Getting Very High or Drunk on Alcohol in Year Prior to Initial Interview	.130	.137	.345****	
Psychosocial, Offense, & Abuse-Neglect History Rotated Factors:				
Varimax Factor 1	.307	.147	.321****	
Varimax Factor 2	.098	.047	.051	
Varimax Factor 3	.240	.115*	.107*	
Varimax Factor 4	.058	.028	.051	
Varimax Factor 5	.427	.205****	.212****	
Varimax Factor 6	−.150	−.072	−.044	
Varimax Factor 7	.153	.074	.093	
Varimax Factor 8	.012	.006	−.006	0.213 (F = 4.72**** df = 15,262)
Group assignment (FEI)	−.195	−.047	−.052	0.002 (F = 0.69 df = 1,261)
Residualized Variable comparing FEI completed vs. FEI non-completed cases	−.708	−.114**	−.114**	0.013 (F = 4.38** df = 1,260)
Constant	0.760			Overall R^2 = 0.228 F for R^2 = 4.51**** df = 17,260

servation. The Year 1 predictor variables, including the youths' Year 1 reported frequency of getting very high or drunk on alcohol, had $R^2 = 0.213$ (F = 4.72; df = 15,262; p < .001). The R^2 change value (0.002) associated with the FEI-ESI group assignment variable was not statistically significant. However, the R^2 change associated with the residualized variable comparing FEI completed and FEI non-completed youths (.013) was statistically significant (F = 4.38; df = 1,260; p < .05). Compared to FEI non-completed youths, FEI completed youths reported getting very high or drunk on alcohol less often. Overall, all the predictor variables accounted for 22.8 percent of the variance (F = 4.51; df = 17,260; p < .001).

Predicting Self-Reported Frequency of Marijuana/Hashish Use Since Initial Interview

Table 21 displays the results of a stepwise regression analysis predicting the youths' reported frequency of marijuana/hashish use at last observation. The R^2 of the Year 1 predictor variables, including the youths' lifetime frequency of marijuana/hashish use reported at initial interview, is 0.304 (F = 7.64; df = 15,262; p < .001). The R^2 change reflecting FEI or ESI group assignment (0.001) was not statistically significant. The residualized variable comparing FEI completed youths and FEI non-completed youths increased R^2 by .003, which was nonsignificant. Overall, the predictor variables accounted for 30.8 percent of the variance (F = 6.81; df = 17,260; p < .001).

Predicting Recent Use of Marijuana/Hashish and Cocaine at Follow-Up Interview as Determined by RIAH® Test Results

Since the RIAH® test results are dichotomous, separate stepwise logistic regression analyses were performed to identify the factors predicting the youths' recent use of these two drugs at the time of their last observation (Hanushek & Jackson, 1997; Demaris, 1992; Menard, 1995). In each analysis, the Year 1 counterpart of the last observation hair test drug result being predicted was included among the predictor variables.

Predicting Marijuana Use

The results of the stepwise logistic regression analysis predicting marijuana use at last observation for the 213 youths with RIAH® test results for this drug are presented in Table 22. The Year 1 predictors were significantly associated with follow-up marijuana use (chi-square = 49.102; df = 15; p < .001). The chi-square change relating to FEI or ESI group assignment was not statistically significant. The chi-square change associated with the residualized variable comparing FEI completed and FEI non-completed youths was also nonsignificant.

Predicting Cocaine Use

A stepwise logistic regression analysis was completed to identify the predictors of the youths' RIAH® test results for cocaine at last observation. The

☐ **Table 21: Regression and Correlation Coefficients of Self-Reported Frequency of Marijuana/Hashish Use (n = 278)**

Variables	b	(beta)	r	R² change
Age	−.225	−.123**	.017	
Race (Black)	−.450	−.076	−.069	
Gender (male)	.389	.066	.100*	
Ethnicity (Hispanic)	−.230	−.034	−.013	
Living situation (living with mother)	.517	.088*	.085	
Case Type (Arbitration/JASP)	−.011	−.002	−.210****	
Self-Reported Lifetime Frequency of Marijuana/Hashish Use Prior to Initial Interview	.367	.231**	.456****	
Psychosocial, Offense, & Abuse-Neglect History Rotated Factors:				
Varimax Factor 1	.612	.209**	.365****	
Varimax Factor 2	.183	.063	.051	
Varimax Factor 3	.540	.184***	.242****	
Varimax Factor 4	−.012	−.004	.022	
Varimax Factor 5	.509	.174***	.209****	
Varimax Factor 6	.086	.029	.055	
Varimax Factor 7	.169	.058	.104*	
Varimax Factor 8	−.297	−.101*	−.127**	0.304
				(F = 7.64****
				(df = 15,262)
Group assignment (FEI)	−.206	−.035	−.034	0.001
				(F = 0.44
				df = 1,261)
Residualized Variable comparing FEI completed vs. FEI non-completed cases	−.441	−.051	−.051	0.003
				(F = 0.97
				df = 1,260)
Constant	6.097			Overall R² = 0.308
				F for R² = 6.81****
				df = 17,260

results of this analysis are shown in Table 23. The Year 1 predictors were significantly associated with last observation cocaine use (chi-square = 56.02; df = 15; p < .001). The low chi-square change associated with FEI or ESI group assignment indicated group assignment was not significantly related to this outcome variable. Further, the chi-square change associated with the residualized variable comparing FEI completed and FEI non-completed youths was not significant.

□ Table 22: Logistic Regression Model of Hair Test Results for Marijuana (n = 213)[†]

Predictors	Coefficient	Standard Error	Odds Ratio	Model Chi-Square (Improvement over Null Model)
Age	.262	.115	1.300	
Race (Black)	.224	.449	.280	
Gender (male)	.211	.375	.260	
Ethnicity (Hispanic)	−.281	.415	.212	
Living situation (living with mother)	.080	.343	.087	
Case Type (Arbitration/JASP)	−.618	.375	.333	
Hair Test Results for Marijuana at Initial Interview	1.424	.712	4.153	
Psychosocial, Offense, & Abuse-Neglect History Rotated Factors:				
Varimax Factor 1	.110	.201	1.116	
Varimax Factor 2	−.072	.176	.930	
Varimax Factor 3	.053	.279	1.055	
Varimax Factor 4	.487	.300	1.628	
Varimax Factor 5	.206	.205	1.229	
Varimax Factor 6	.105	.180	1.111	
Varimax Factor 7	.285	.206	1.330	
Varimax Factor 8	−.212	.196	.809	49.102**** df = 15
Group assignment (FEI)	−.421	.340	.276	1.60 df = 1 p = .103 (n.s.)
Residualized Variable comparing FEI completed vs. FEI non-completed cases	−.148	.480	.095	0.10 df = 1 p = n.s.
Constant	−3.906			

† 26 cases were missing information on their initial interview marijuana hair test results (most often due to quantity not sufficient for testing). The missing data were replaced by the mean of this variable to retain as many cases as possible in the analyses. The hair test results were coded as follows: Negative = 0; Positive = 1.

Time and Treatment Group by Time Effects on the Psychosocial Outcome Measures

Additional regression analyses for each of the outcome measures were performed to determine the effect of length of follow-up time and to separately assess the interaction between the variable reflecting completion of the FEI

□ **Table 23: Logistic Regression Model of Hair Test Results for Cocaine (n = 235)[†]**

Predictors	Coefficient	Standard Error	Odds Ratio	Model Chi-Square (Improvement over Null Model)
Age	.005	.119	1.005	
Race (Black)	1.139	.465	3.559	
Gender (male)	.676	.390	1.330	
Ethnicity (Hispanic)	.448	.465	.700	
Living situation (living with mother)	−.399	.358	.268	
Case Type (Arbitration/JASP)	.305	.394	.414	
Hair Test Results for Cocaine at Initial Interview	.618	.597	1.856	
Psychosocial, Offense, & Abuse-Neglect History Rotated Factors:				
Varimax Factor 1	−.011	.205	.989	
Varimax Factor 2	−.340	.195	.711	
Varimax Factor 3	.654	.257	1.924	
Varimax Factor 4	.092	.213	1.097	
Varimax Factor 5	.286	.198	1.331	
Varimax Factor 6	.205	.185	1.228	
Varimax Factor 7	−.279	.203	.756	
Varimax Factor 8	−.236	.193	.790	56.02****
				df = 15
Group assignment (FEI)	−.039	.346	.038	0.01
				df = 1
Residualized Variable comparing FEI completed vs. FEI non-completed cases	−.159	.496	.853	0.10
				df = 1
Constant	−0.056			

† Six cases were missing information on their initial interview hair test results. The missing data were replaced by the mean of this variable to retain as many cases as possible in the analyses. The hair test results were coded as follows: Negative = 0; Positive = 1.

versus non-completion of the FEI and follow-up length. The results of these analyses indicated the following: (1) statistically significant reductions in self-reported general theft crimes, crimes against persons, and total delinquency over time, and (2) no significant completion of the FEI versus non-completion of the FEI by follow-up length interaction effects were found–with one slight exception. For total delinquency, FEI completers had lower rates of reported involvement in total delinquency than FEI non-completers at Year 2 and Year 4, but the two groups had equal rates of reported involvement in total delinquency at Year 3. According to the interaction analyses, with one slight exception, youths completing the FEI had consistently better outcomes over time in regard to reported frequency of getting very high or drunk on alcohol, claimed involvement in crimes against persons, drug sales, and total delinquency.

The Influence of Change of Project Clinical Leadership on Self-Report Psychosocial Outcome Data

The clinical leadership of the project changed in April 1996, at which time the clinical director was replaced by a clinical coordinator and two line supervisors. Hence, a dummy coded variable was created, reflecting whether families entered the project prior to (0) or subsequent to (1) March 1996. This variable was incorporated in four additional stepwise regression analyses on outcomes with previously reported significant results: (1) self-reported crimes against persons, (2) self-reported drug sales, (3) self-reported total delinquency, and (4) self-reported frequency of getting very high or drunk on alcohol. These analyses indicated this time-of-entry-into-the project variable *did not* have an appreciable effect on the results we reported earlier. (Tables reporting these findings are available from the senior author upon request.)

DISCUSSION AND CONCLUSIONS

Overall, the results of our analyses indicate that youths completing the FEI had significantly lower reported rates of getting very high or drunk on alcohol, crimes against persons, drug sales, and total delinquency, than youths not completing the FEI. These results took into account group differences on a wide variety of demographic, psychosocial, offense history, and abuse-neglect history variables. In addition, the findings held up under further study of possible interaction effects. These four hypothesis-consistent, significant effects exceed the less than one such effect one could, on average, expect on the basis of chance alone if outcomes were uncorrelated; they provide evidence in support of the efficacy and sustained effect of the Family Empowerment Intervention. Although statistically significant, the intervention accounts for under two percent of the variation in any dependent variable. Abelson (1985) has suggested that the proportion of variation may not be a useful measure of the importance of a predictor.

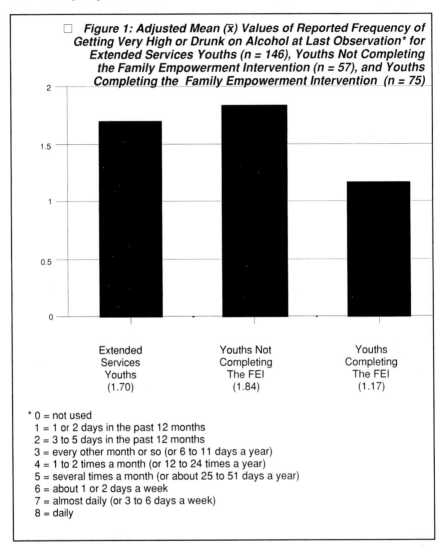

☐ *Figure 1: Adjusted Mean (x̄) Values of Reported Frequency of Getting Very High or Drunk on Alcohol at Last Observation* for Extended Services Youths (n = 146), Youths Not Completing the Family Empowerment Intervention (n = 57), and Youths Completing the Family Empowerment Intervention (n = 75)*

Extended Services Youths (1.70)

Youths Not Completing The FEI (1.84)

Youths Completing The FEI (1.17)

* 0 = not used
1 = 1 or 2 days in the past 12 months
2 = 3 to 5 days in the past 12 months
3 = every other month or so (or 6 to 11 days a year)
4 = 1 to 2 times a month (or 12 to 24 times a year)
5 = several times a month (or about 25 to 51 days a year)
6 = about 1 or 2 days a week
7 = almost daily (or 3 to 6 days a week)
8 = daily

An alternative explanation for our findings is that youths did better because they were amenable to intervention, rather than as the effect of the intervention. However, if this were the case, one would expect that there would be other differences in Year 1 characteristics, which was not the case. Neither FEI vs. ESI youths nor FEI completers vs. FEI non-completers differed significantly on the Year 1 characteristics (FEI vs. ESI, chi-squared test of Wilks's

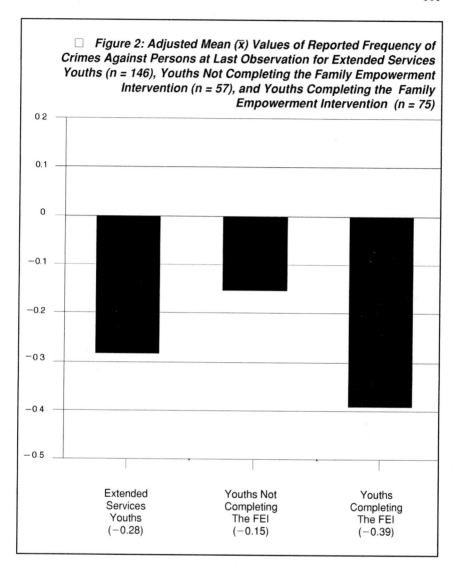

Figure 2: Adjusted Mean (x̄) Values of Reported Frequency of Crimes Against Persons at Last Observation for Extended Services Youths (n = 146), Youths Not Completing the Family Empowerment Intervention (n = 57), and Youths Completing the Family Empowerment Intervention (n = 75)

lambda = 14.47, df = 14, p = n.s.; FEI completers vs. non-completers, chi-squared test of Wilks' lambda = 9.76, df = 14, p = n.s.)

These important effects are presented in more visible fashion in Figures 1 to 4, which display the mean values at last observation for reported frequency of getting very high or drunk on alcohol (Figure 1), reported crimes against persons (Figure 2), reported frequency of drug sales (Figure 3), and reported total

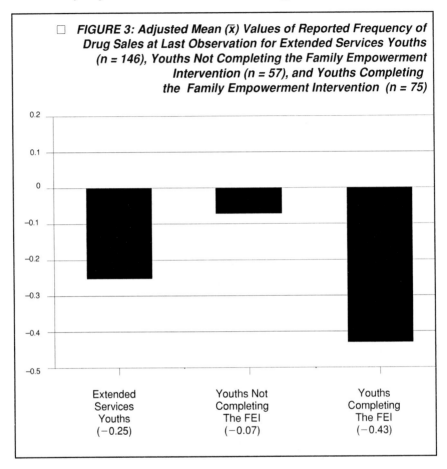

□ **FIGURE 3: Adjusted Mean (x̄) Values of Reported Frequency of Drug Sales at Last Observation for Extended Services Youths (n = 146), Youths Not Completing the Family Empowerment Intervention (n = 57), and Youths Completing the Family Empowerment Intervention (n = 75)**

delinquency (Figure 4). In each case, youths completing the FEI had lower rates of these behaviors than ESI youths or youths not completing the intervention.

The long-term effects of the FEI are less robust than the 12-month impact of the intervention on the youths' psychosocial functioning (see: Dembo, Seeberger, Shemwell, Schmeidler, Klein, Rollie, Pacheco, Hartsfield, & Wothke, in press). Since the intervention was designed to be short-term, and no additional services were systematically applied following completion of the FEI, the long-term outcome effects we found were gratifying. We believe the strength of the *sustained effect* of the intervention could have been enhanced by periodic booster sessions designed to support target youths and family maintenance of their intervention gains.

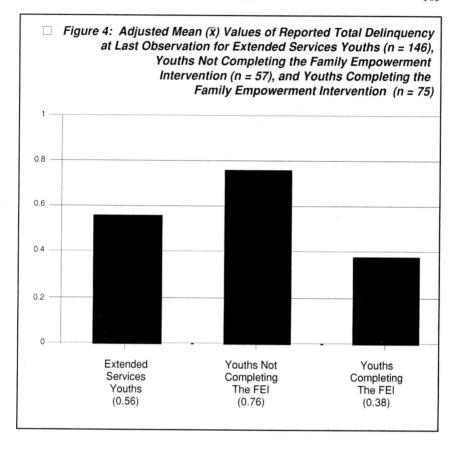

Figure 4: Adjusted Mean (x̄) Values of Reported Total Delinquency at Last Observation for Extended Services Youths (n = 146), Youths Not Completing the Family Empowerment Intervention (n = 57), and Youths Completing the Family Empowerment Intervention (n = 75)

At the same time, it is important to note that our findings on the relationships between completing the FEI and lower reported delinquency over time parallel the findings resulting from our study of the long-term impact of the FEI on the youths' recidivism (Dembo, Ramirez-Garnica, Schmeidler, Rollie, Livingston, & Hartsfield, in press). Using official record data, we found that youths who completed the FEI experienced marginally statistically significant lower rates of new charges, and very close to statistically significant fewer new arrests, than other youths involved in the project–covering up to a 48-month follow-up period (cf. Lauritson, 1999).

The long-term psychosocial outcome analyses we completed provide evidence of the *sustained effect* of the FEI on delinquency among youths completing the FEI. These findings are particularly important in light of the experience that the salutary effects of intervention programs for high-risk youths are, unfortunately, often short-lived. The University of Colorado Center for the Study and Prevention of Violence (1999) notes that treatment or intervention gains of most programs are lost after participation in the intervention or soon thereafter. The intervention effects we found are consistent with the main hypothesis of this project. Further, substantial justice system direct cost savings can be anticipated by use of this intervention (see: Dembo, Ramirez-Garnica, Rollie, Schmeidler, Livingston, & Hartsfield, in press). We hope the continued documented value of this attractive, cost-efficient intervention will encourage its implementation in other jurisdictions.

REFERENCES

Abelson, R.P. (1985). A variance explanation paradox: When a little is a lot. *Psychological Bulletin, 97*, 129-133.

Alexander, J.F., & Parsons, B.V. (1982). *Functional Family Therapy: Principles and Procedures*. Carmel, CA: Brooks/Cole.

Arcia, E., Keyes, L., Gallagher, J.J., & Herrick, H. (1993). National portrait of sociodemographic factors associated with underutilization of services: Relevance to early intervention. *Journal of Early Intervention, 17*, 283-297.

Baumgartner, W., & Hill, V. (1996). Hair analysis for organic analyses: Methodology, reliability issues, and field studies. In P. Kintz (ed.), *Drug Testing in Hair*. New York: CRC Press.

Bennett, S., & Bowers, D. (1976). *An Introduction to Multivariate Techniques for Social and Behavioral Sciences*. New York: John Wiley & Sons.

Bronfenbrenner, U. (1979). *The Ecology of Human Development: Experiments by Nature and Design*. Cambridge, MA: Harvard University Press.

Cervenka, K.A., Dembo, R., & Brown, C.H. (1996). A Family Empowerment Intervention for families of juvenile offenders. *Aggression and Violent Behavior, 1*, 205-216.

Christenson, A., & Jacobson, N.S. (1994). Who (or what) can do psychotherapy: The status and challenge of non-professional therapies. *Psychological Science, 5*, 8-14.

Demaris, A. (1992). *Logit Modeling: Practical Applications*. Newbury Park, CA: Sage.

Dembo, R., & Brown, R. (1994). The Hillsborough County Juvenile Assessment Center. *Journal of Child and Adolescent Substance Abuse, 3*, 25-43.

Dembo, R., Pacheco, K., Schmeidler, J., Fisher, L., & Cooper, S. (1997). Drug use and delinquent behavior among high risk youths. *Journal of Child and Adolescent Substance Abuse, 6*, 1-25.

Dembo, R., Ramirez-Garnica, G., Rollie, M., Schmeidler, J., Livingston, S., & Harstfield, A. (In press). Youth recidivism 12 months after a Family Empowerment Intervention: Final Report. *Journal of Offender Rehabilitation*.

Dembo, R., Ramirez-Garnica, G., Schmeidler, J., Rollie, M., Livingston, S., & Harstfield, A. (2001). Long-term impact of a family empowerment intervention on juvenile offender recidivism. *Journal of Offender Rehabilitation 33(1)*.

Dembo, R., Seeberger, W., Shemwell, M., Schmeidler, J., Klein, L., Rollie, M., Pacheco, K., Hartsfield, A., & Wothke, W. (in press). Psychosocial functioning among juvenile offenders 12 months after family empowerment intervention. *Journal of Offender Rehabilitation.*

Dembo, R., Shemwell, M., Guida, J., Schmeidler, J., Pacheco, K., & Seeberger, W. (1998). A longitudinal study of the impact of a Family Empowerment Intervention on juvenile offender psychosocial functioning: A first assessment. *Journal of Child and Adolescent Substance Abuse, 8,* 15-54.

Dembo, R., Williams, L., Berry, E., Getreu, A., Washburn, M., Wish, E.D., & Schmeidler, J. (1990). Examination of the relationships among drug use, emotional/psychological problems and crime among youths entering a juvenile detention center. *International Journal of the Addictions, 25,* 1301-1340.

Dembo, R., Williams, L., & Schmeidler, J. (1998). Key findings of the Tampa longitudinal study of juvenile detainees: Contributions to a theory of drug use and delinquency among high risk youths. In A.R. Roberts (ed.), *Juvenile Justice: Policies, Programs and Services.* 2nd edition. Chicago: Nelson-Hall.

Dembo, R., Williams, L., Schmeidler, J., & Howitt, D. (1991). *Tough Cases: School Outreach for At-Risk Youth.* Washington, DC: US Department of Education, Office of the Assistant Secretary for Educational Research and Improvement.

Dembo, R., Williams, L., Wothke, W., Schmeidler, J., & Brown, C.H. (1992). The role of family factors, physical abuse and sexual victimization experiences in high risk youths' alcohol and other drug use and delinquency: A longitudinal model. *Violence and Victims, 7,* 245-266.

Dembo, R., Wothke, W., Shemwell, M., Pacheco, K., Seeberger, W., Rollie, M., & Schmeidler, J. (In press). The relationships of high risk youth family problems and their problem behavior: A structural model. *Journal of Child and Adolescent Substance Abuse.*

Derogatis, L.D. (1983). *SCL-90-R Administration, Scoring and Procedures Manual.* Towson, MD: Clinical Psychometric Research.

Draper, N.R., & Smith, H. (1980). *Applied Regression Analysis,* 2nd ed. New York: Wiley.

Elliott, D.S., Ageton, S.S., Huizinga, D., Knowles, B.A., & Canter, R.J. (1983). *The Prevalence and Incidence of Delinquent Behavior: 1976-1980.* Boulder, CO: Behavioral Research Institute.

Finkelhor, D. (1979). *Sexually Victimized Children.* New York: Free Press.

Fishburn, P.M., Abelson, H.I., & Cisin, I. (1980). *National Survey on Drug Abuse: Main Findings-1979.* Rockville, MD: National Institute on Drug Abuse.

Hanushek, E.A., & Jackson, J.E. (1977). *Statistical Methods for Social Scientists.* New York: Academic Press.

Henggeler, S.W., & Borduin, C.M. (1990). *Family Therapy and Beyond: A Multisystemic Approach to Treating the Behavior Problems of Children and Adolescents.* Pacific Grove, CA: Brooks/Cole.

Henggeler, S.W., Melton, G.B., Smith, L.A., Schoenwald, S.W., & Hanley, J.H. (1993). Family preservation using multi-systemic treatment: Long term follow-up to a clinical trial with serious juvenile offenders. *Journal of Child and Family Studies, 2,* 283-293.

Henggeler, S.W., Schoenwald, S.K., Pickrel, S.G., Brondino, M.J., Borduin, C.M., & Hall, J.A. (1994). *Treatment Manual for Family Preservation Using Multisystemic Therapy.* Charleston, SC: Medical University of South Carolina.

Kim, J., & Mueller, C.E. (1978). *Factor Analysis: Statistical Methods and Practical Issues.* Beverly Hills, CA: Sage.

Klecka, W.R. (1980). *Discriminant Analysis.* Beverly Hills, CA: Sage.

Klitzner, M., Fisher, D., Stewart, K., & Gilbert, S. (1991). *Report to the Robert Wood Johnson Foundation on Strategies for Early Intervention with Children and Youth to Avoid Abuse of Addictive Substances.* Bethesda, MD: Pacific Institute for Research and Evaluation.

Kumpfer, K., & Alvarado, R. (1998). *Effective Family Strengthening Interventions.* Washington, DC: U.S. Department of Justice. NCJ 171121.

Lauritson, J.L. (1999). Limitation in the use of longitudinal self-report data: A comment. *Criminology, 37,* 687-694.

McBride, D., Vanderwall, C., Terry, Y., & Van Buren, H. (1999). *Breaking the Cycle of Drug Use Among Juvenile Offenders.* Report prepared for the National Institute of Justice. Berrien Springs, MI: Andrews U., Dept. of Behavioral Sciences.

Menard, S. (1995). *Applied Logistic Regression Analysis.* Thousand Oaks, CA: Sage.

Mouzakitis, C.W. (1981). Inquiry into the problem of child abuse and juvenile delinquency. In R.J. Hunner & Y.E. Walker (eds.), *Exploring the Relationship Between Child Abuse and Delinquency.* Montclair, NJ: Allenheld, Osmun and Co.

Office of National Drug Control Policy (1997). *What America's Users Spend on Illegal Drugs, 1988-1995.* Washington, DC: ONDCP.

Rahdert, E., & Czechowicz, D. (Eds.) (1995). *Adolescent Drug Abuse: Clinical Assessment and Therapeutic Interventions.* Rockville, MD: National Institute on Drug Abuse.

Sherman, L., Gottfredson, D., MacKenzie, D., Eck, J., Reuten, P., & Bushway, S. (1997). *Preventing Crime: What Works, What Doesn't, What's Promising?* College Park, MD: University of Maryland, Dept. of Criminology and Criminal Justice.

Sirles, E.A. (1990). Dropout from intake, diagnostics, and treatment. *Community Mental Health Journal, 26,* 345-360.

Straus, M.A. (1979). Measuring intrafamily conflict and violence: The conflict tactics (CT) scales. *Journal of Marriage and the Family, 41,* 75-88.

Straus, M.A. (1983). Ordinary violence, child abuse, and wife-beating, What do they have in common? In D. Finkelhor, R.J. Gelles, G.T. Hotaling, & M.A. Straus (eds.), *The Dark Side of Families: Current Family Violence Research.* Beverly Hills, CA: Sage.

Straus, M.A., Gelles, R.J., & Steinmetz, S.K. (1980). *Behind Closed Doors: Violence in the American Family.* New York: Doubleday/Anchor.

Straus, M., Hamby, S.L., Finkelhor, D., Moore, D., & Runyan, D. (1998). Identification of child maltreatment with parent-child Conflict Tactics Scales: Development and psychometric data for a national sample of American parents. *Child Abuse and Neglect, 22,* 249-270.

Substance Abuse and Mental Health Services Administration (SAMHSA) (1997). *Preliminary Data from the 1996 National Household Survey on Drug Abuse.* Rockville, MD: SAMHSA.

Szapocznik, J., & Kurtines, W.M. (1989). *Breakthroughs in Family Therapy with Drug-Abusing and Problem Youth.* New York: Springer Publishing Co.

Teplin, L.A., & Swartz, J. (1989). Screening for severe mental disorder in jails: The development of the referral decision scale. *Law and Human Behavior, 13,* 1-18.

Tolan, P., Ryan, K., & Jaffe, C. (1988). Adolescents' mental health service use and provider, process, and recipient characteristics. *Journal of Clinical Child Psychology, 17*, 229-236.

University of Colorado Center for the Study and Prevention of Violence Model Program Selection Criteria. (1999). Available FTP: 128.138.129.25. File: www.colorado.edu/cspu/blueprints/about/criteria.htm.

Weisz, J.R., Weiss, B., Han, S.S., Granger, D.A., & Norton, B. (1995). Effects of psychotherapy with children and adolescents revisited: A meta-analysis of treatment outcome studies. *Psychological Bulletin, 117*, 450-468.

AUTHORS' NOTES

Richard Dembo, PhD, is a professor of Criminology at the University of South Florida in Tampa. He has a long-term interest in developing, implementing and evaluating intervention programs for high-risk youths.

James Schmeidler, PhD, is an assistant clinical professor in the Department of Psychiatry and Biomathematical Sciences at the Mt. Sinai School of Medicine. He has considerable experience applying statistical procedures to behavioral science data.

William Seeberger, BA, is a research assistant in the Department of Criminology at the University of South Florida. His research interests relate to interventions involving high-risk youths.

Marina Shemwell, BA, is an administrative assistant/research associate to the Youth Support Project. She is employed by the Agency for Community Treatment Services, Inc. Her research interests relate to evaluating interventions for high-risk youths.

Matthew Rollie, BS, is a graduate assistant in the Department of Criminology at the University of South Florida. He is currently a student at the University of South Florida College of Public Health in the Department of Environmental Health and is working on his master's degree in Tropical Public Health/Infectious Diseases.

Kimberly Pacheco, BA, was an administrative assistant/research associate on the Youth Support Project. Her research interests centered on services for high-risk youths.

Stephen Livingston, BA, is a research assistant in the Department of Criminology at the University of South Florida. He has been associated with the Youth Support Project since 1998.

Werner Wothke, PhD, is the president of SmallWaters Corporation, which publishes and supports multivariate software programs, including AMOS (Analysis of Moment Structures). He is an expert in multivariate analysis procedures and in psychosocial measurement.

The preparation of this manuscript was supported by Grant #1-RO1-DA08707, funded by the National Institute on Drug Abuse. The authors are grateful for their support. However, the research results reported and the views expressed in the article do not necessarily imply any policy or research endorsement by our funding agency.

The authors would like to thank clinical, intervention, and other research staff for their contributions to this project. Great thanks are due to project Field Consultants for their work. The authors deeply appreciate the support of Mr. Darrell Manning, supervisor of the Juvenile Assessment Center; he was a great resource to the work. Ms. Laine Klein was extremely helpful in completing interviews for this project. The authors also deeply appreciate Ms. Marianne Bell's word processing of this manuscript.

Address correspondence to Richard Dembo, PhD, Criminology Department, University of South Florida, 4202 E. Fowler Avenue, Tampa, FL 33620.

APPENDIX A
Juvenile Court Referral Reasons, by Category

Violent Felonies

Murder/manslaughter
Attempted murder/manslaughter
Sexual battery
Other felonious sex offenses
Armed robbery
Other robbery
Aggravated assault and/or battery

Violent Misdemeanors

Assault and/or battery (not aggravated)

Public Disorder Misdemeanors

Disorderly conduct (trespassing, loitering, and prowling)

Drug Misdemeanors

Misdemeanor violation of drug laws (excluding marijuana)
Misdemeanor marijuana offense
Possession of alcoholic beverage
Other alcohol offense

Physical Abuse

Skull fracture/brain damage/subdural hematoma
Internal injuries
Bone fracture
Sprain/dislocation
Bruises/welts
Cuts/punctures/bites
Burns/scalds
Asphyxiation/suffocation/drowning
Intentional poisoning
Confinement/bizarre punishment
Excessive corporal punishment/beatings (injury unknown)
Other physical abuse

Sexual Abuse

Sexual battery (incest)
Sexual battery (no incest)
Fondling/other sexual abuse
Sexual exploitation–child pornography
Other sexual exploitation (including prostitution)

Property Felonies

Arson
Burglary (breaking and entering)
Auto theft
Grand larceny (excluding auto theft)
Receiving stolen property

Drug Felonies

Felony violation of drug laws (excluding marijuana)
Felony marijuana offense

Property Misdemeanors

Petty larceny (excluding retail theft)
Retail theft (shoplifting)
Receiving stolen property (under $100)
Criminal mischief (vandalism)

Neglect

Malnutrition/deprived of food
Failure to thrive
Deprived of clothing
Deprived of shelter
Medical neglect
Failure to provide medical care (religious reasons)
Unattended/unsupervised conditions hazardous to health
Abandonment
Other neglect

Mental Injury

Emotional abuse
Emotional neglect

Status Offenses

Local (intracounty) runaway
Runaway from other Florida county
Out of state runaway
Truancy
Beyond control

Source: Florida Department of Health and Rehabilitative Services, Children, Youth and Families, Client Information System: Selected Elements and Codes for Intake Staff.

APPENDIX B

Communalities and Loading of the Various Time 1 Psychosocial, Offense History, and Abuse-Neglect History Variables on the Eight Rotated Varimax Components (n = 278)*

Variable	Rotated Varimax Factor								Communality
	1	2	3	4	5	6	7	8	
Lifetime reported use of marijuana	.701	.046	.261	.289	.202	.050	.173	−.112	.73
Lifetime reported use of hallucinogens	.800	.005	−.027	−.068	−.172	.003	.008	.178	.71
Lifetime reported use of cocaine	.753	−.041	−.131	.072	−.044	.001	−.044	.227	.67
Self-reported frequency of getting very high/drunk on alcohol in past year	.766	.160	.013	.111	.146	.001	.066	−.124	.66
RIAH® test results for marijuana	.191	.148	.661	.243	−.223	.068	.069	−.182	.65
RIAH® test results for cocaine	.066	.158	.505	.423	−.001	−.095	−.211	.115	.53
Referral history for drug offenses	.068	−.108	−.045	.717	.053	.170	.217	−.132	.63
Friends' alcohol/other drug use	.758	.221	.068	−.032	.030	.006	.034	−.200	.67
Family alcohol/other drug and mental health problems	.200	.669	−.070	−.064	−.105	.103	−.013	.046	.52
Friends' involvement with the justice system	.055	.028	.196	.256	.425	.247	.101	.046	.36
Family involvement with the justice system	.019	.032	.036	.129	.734	−.122	−.083	−.049	.58
Referral history for violence, property, and public disorder offenses	.082	−.210	.625	−.106	.380	.078	.166	.150	.65
Arrest charges for property offenses upon entering JAC	−.016	.042	−.074	−.095	.137	.722	−.110	−.096	.58
Arrest charges for violent offenses upon entering JAΨ	2.062	.007	−.025	−.082	.137	−.795	.033	−.102	.67
Self-reported delinquency in past year	.498	.243	.148	−.082	.459	.150	.133	.090	.60
Self-reported sexual victimization	.260	.471	.131	.050	.142	−.157	−.016	−.308	.45
Self-reported being hit or beaten	.073	.134	.094	.038	.013	−.006	.020	.738	.58
Self-reported serious physical abuse	.043	.555	−.098	.028	.157	.068	.515	−.087	.62
Referral history for neglect	−.116	−.011	.553	−.142	.190	−.094	−.038	.101	.40
Referral history for physical abuse	.005	−.043	.106	.047	.076	−.112	.809	.197	.73
SCL−90−R score	−.010	.658	.113	.014	.072	−.029	.047	.322	.56
Educational lag	−.049	−.030	−.020	−.665	−.175	.168	.168	−.159	.56
Mental health treatment (ever)	.164	.110	−.060	−.055	−.179	−.082	.416	−.191	.29
Rotation Sums of Squared Loadings	3.32	1.69	1.62	1.45	1.42	1.40	1.34	1.16	

*For each variable, missing values are replaced by the variable mean.

Index